the JOY *of* PRIESTHOOD

the JOY *of* PRIESTHOOD

Fr. Stephen J. Rossetti

ave maria press AmP Notre Dame, Indiana

Nihil Obstat:

Rev. Andrew E. Baranski

Censor Deputatus

Imprimatur:

Most Rev. James M. Moynihan

Bishop of Syracuse, New York

Given at Syracuse, New York, on December 30, 2004

www.avemariapress.com

ISBN-10 1-59471-066-X ISBN-13 978-1-59471-066-7

Cover by Brian Conley

Text design by Katherine Robinson Coleman

Printed and bound in the United States of America.

Library of Congress Cataloging-in-Publication Data

Rossetti, Stephen J., 1951-

The joy of priesthood / Stephen J. Rossetti.

p. cm.

Includes bibliographical references.

ISBN 1-59471-066-X (pbk.)

1. Catholic Church—Clergy. 2. Priesthood—Catholic Church. I. Title.

BX1912.R675 2005

253'.2'088282—dc22

2005010274

Acknowledgements

I am grateful to Bishop John McCormack, Fr. Ed Arsenault, Fr. Bill Parent, Fr. Ed Bodnar, and Fr. Lou Cameli for reading the manuscript and for their many excellent suggestions. I was blessed to have such fine readers.

I am grateful for the fraternal support of my *Jesu Caritas* brothers: Fr. Dan Coughlin, Fr. Clete Kiley, Fr. Bill Parent, and Msgr. Peter Vaghi.

I am grateful to my bishops of the Diocese of Syracuse, Bishop James Moynihan and Bishop Thomas Costello. Their ready encouragement and ongoing support have been a great blessing for me.

I am grateful to Nancy Farran who has been a kind and dedicated coworker. She has helped to make this book possible.

As always, I am particularly grateful to my mother, Helene Rossetti. She is the best editor an author could have.

Dedicated to

our priests,

living and deceased,

with gratitude.

Contents

Foreword

"Joy," claims French philosopher Leon Bloy, "is the infallible sign of God's presence."

One would thus look for a palpable spirit of joy in those very men called by the Church to be "signs of God's presence," her priests. And, if recent studies are correct, priests are indeed happy men: Over 90 percent of them report high satisfaction with their call and their ministry and "would do it all again" if the calendar were turned back. That's very good news.

The bad news is that, according to the same research, the public *perception* is that priests are not joyful, that the priesthood is in a life-threatening crisis, and that many priests, while internally happy, come off as crabs and malcontents.

Lord knows there are abundant reasons for this: the horror and heavy weight of the abuse scandal, the carping from fringes on both the left and right, and the declining numbers of clergy. It is very tough to be a good and faithful priest, yet the great majority are, and almost all are happy.

Father Stephen Rossetti, a most effective and happy priest of the presbyterate of the Diocese of Syracuse, and the president of the Saint Luke Institute, dedicated to the healing of hurting, sick, and struggling priests, has a fifty-yard line seat on the priesthood. He is in a unique position to speak to his brother priests and to the millions who care about them, about the "joy of priesthood."

The book you are about to begin will not let you down. Father Rossetti deftly describes the nobility of the priestly call, yet also all that degrades it; he tells us eloquently of the triumph of grace, yet also of the crushing potency of sin; he lets us know why priests smile so much, yet also why you will at times catch them crying; he tells us what makes effective priests tick, and what destroys others.

Any priest who wants to appreciate more fully the power of his call and his identity, while realistically reassessing the temptations and perils he faces, will thank Father Rossetti for this timely, compelling spiritual reading. Anyone who loves the Church and her priests will benefit as well from this perceptive treatment of "those mysterious priests," as Fulton Sheen described them thirty years ago.

And we will all come away more firmly convinced of the classical Catholic dictum that "grace builds on nature." For what Father Rossetti valiantly believes is that the unfailing power, awe, mercy, and strength of the grace of holy orders, blended with the wholesome, healthy, self-knowing, mature nature of a man humbly open to that grace, produces a chemistry that combines God and man, heaven and earth, saint and sinner, rise and fall, life and death—*a priest,* a man of joy.

✠ TIMOTHY M. DOLAN, Archbishop of Milwaukee
Chairman, Bishops' Committee on
Priestly Life and Ministry
March 24, 2005, Feast of St. John Vianney,
Year of the Eucharist

Introduction

This book has been written over a period of fifteen years, during which I have been working with priests who suffer with psychological and spiritual problems. They have taught me much and I gladly share what I have learned from and with them.

Over these fifteen years, each of these chapters has slowly taken shape, beginning as articles and talks. The ideas therein have been gradually refined and integrated, and now they comprise a unified reflection on the priesthood.

Sometimes people ask me if ministering to priests in difficulty discourages me or assails my love for the priesthood or the Church. Of course, there are moments when I feel upset by what I have heard or I am saddened by their grief. If I lose the ability to be touched by genuine tragedy or if I am no longer angered by egregious behavior, then I have overstayed in this work. But, such moments have been fully overshadowed by a stronger grace.

I have grown in my admiration for our priests. I have been given a stronger love of the priesthood and the Church. In their weakness, these men have shown me the immense dignity of the priesthood and the beauty of the Church. In vulnerability, grace shines more brightly in the human spirit. I have come to know, even more clearly, that the priesthood is a great blessing for the people of God and for those who are its recipients. The laity have instinctively known this truth for centuries. Sometimes we priests forget this reality. We ought never to forget.

This book is meant especially for my brothers, our priests, but I think others might profit from its words. I gladly dedicate this book to our priests with thanks for all they have done. I myself, like other Catholics, owe a special debt of gratitude to some priests in particular, those who have supported me and guided me up close, and those who provided a guiding beacon from afar. As I sit here composing these words, their names and faces cross in front of my mind's eye. I am grateful to God for them and I ask the Blessed Virgin to keep them close to her heart, as I do for all priests.

Many priests speak of Mary in loving, affectionate terms. She is, indeed, Mother of Priests. Her maternal love for priests is the spirit that animates this work and the force that nurtures my own love for them. A priest who has a fervent devotion to her will not stray long or far from the right path. We pray, "Mary, Mother of Priests, intercede for us."

I thank God for our priests and I am grateful for the gift of priesthood. I am especially grateful for having been given the opportunity to journey with many priests in their darkest hour. They have fought with courage and faith. Many have found their way back to health and sanctity. Some are still struggling. The ground we walked together was sacred. It was sanctified by the blood that fell from their pierced hearts and the tears that fell from their eyes. It was in the midst of this struggle that they showed themselves most truly to be priests. It was on this Golgotha of their crucified spirits that we both found the grace of life.

chapter 1

Priesthood Is Difficult

Priesthood is a lot better than I thought it was going to be . . . and a lot tougher.

+ Fr. Frank McNulty

MY BROTHERS IN THE PRIESTHOOD, OUR LIFE IS not easy. Those of you who opted for the more austere monastic orders probably expected a difficult life. Anyone familiar with the life of a Trappist monk or a Carthusian hermit is aware of the commitment to self-denial and penance that these lives entail. On the surface, the life of a priest in ministry looks easier. We have some money in our pockets (not much), the appearances of a bit of freedom, and a life that does not look too ascetical or very rigorous. At one point in our priestly lives most of us have been asked by the laity, "Father, what do you do all day after you say morning Mass?" The implication is that there is not much else tugging at our sleeves once the Mass is over. Nothing could be further from the truth.

Priesthood is difficult. Ironically, we might actually have more vocations to the priesthood if our young people realized how challenging the life really is. Many generous young people want to commit themselves to a life that stretches them and one that, in the end, will mean something. Perhaps this is one of the reasons why the stricter, more traditional religious groups are currently receiving increased vocations. Young people want a life of meaning and challenge. Priesthood, when lived with integrity, is such a life.

One of the greatest asceticisms for priests in active ministry is the asceticism of time. Our time is not our own. The parish priest or chaplain is virtually on call day and night. And people *do* call us. A bereaved parent will call a priest when a child has died. Adult children, painfully watching their parents suffer in the hospital, will ask the priest to visit. The lonely and troubled will look to us for understanding and solace. These needs do not fit into a neat nine to five schedule. At times, it feels to us as if we "don't have a life." By that I mean we do not have much private space or private time. This is true. Giving up control over one's time is a great sacrifice. It is akin to the monk who promises stability, that is, to stay in his monastery for the rest of his life. He, too, loses control over his time and his space.

The demands on our time and energy are relentless and, at times, overwhelming. Every family in the parish has its own story. Each individual experiences moments of joy and moments of sorrow. The longer we spend in a ministry, the more we become involved in their stories. Many invite the priest to share in their lives in little ways, by simply being the recipient of the news outside the church doors after Sunday Mass, or in more extensive ways by walking with the family on their journey. Sharing in the lives of the people whom we serve is one of our greatest joys and it is one of our greatest burdens. If the priest is a caring man at all, he will feel some of the pain of their losses and he will rejoice with them in their moments of joy.

Our life is emotionally intense and rich, but it can also be draining. People do not call us when everything is going fine. They call when they are troubled or when there has been a tragedy. Or they will contact us when there are great joys, someone is about to be married, or they are celebrating the birth of a child. It is not uncommon for a parish priest to preside at a funeral Mass and burial, and then go directly to witness the wedding vows of a young couple followed by a joyous reception. The priest in public ministry lives life in its intensity.

In this life, we are constantly reminded of our limits and of the flood of human needs everywhere around us. There is simply no way that we can respond to all the needs out there, including many requests that are truly legitimate. Survey research has consistently shown that priests struggle with their workloads. In a 2001 study sponsored by the National Federation of Priests' Councils (NFPC), the second and third problems most often endorsed by priests were "too much work" and "unrealistic demands and expectations of lay people."[1] Ministry has always been a bottomless pit. But the bottomless pit has become even more foreboding with the declining numbers of priests in the prosperous nations of the world and increasing numbers of Catholics. I conducted my own survey of priests from September 2003 to January 2005. There were 1,172 priests surveyed from 15 dioceses across the U.S.[2] The survey showed that 42.9 percent agreed with the statement: "I feel overwhelmed with the amount of work I have to do." That's a lot of priests.

This, too, is a form of asceticism we must endure: feeling our limits. We cannot say yes to all because ministry is a bottomless pit. We priests want to be thought of as nice guys and we find it a pleasure to say yes. It is painful to say no or not to respond to valid human needs when there is no time. It is an asceticism to say no. Each day, the priest makes the difficult discernment of deciding which needs he can fulfill and which ones he cannot. Frankly, some are not doing this well and many are overextending themselves in the process. This is a challenge we must face personally and collectively. Our priests need assistance in setting appropriate limits.

I recall a priest from South America visiting a parish in the United States. He was surprised to see the priest attending so many private social functions such as wedding and baptismal receptions. He remarked, "In my town there is one priest for 50,000 people. I cannot attend private functions. I am only able to go to social functions when the entire community is present, like great feast days." Perhaps we can learn from our brothers in other countries. We must engage in the painful process of rethinking what it is a priest can and cannot do.

Another asceticism of the priest in ministry is the loneliness of uniqueness. The priest is one who lives among the people. Like them, we are human beings and Christians. Thus there is a common bond that we share. But we are also priests, an office that sets us apart. The priest is their spiritual leader. He is both one of them and always slightly separate. The wearing of clerical or religious garb is a clear sign that we have willingly taken on this yoke of distinctiveness. At times, there is some isolation in this position.

It is important that we priests have other priest friends. It is with them, and usually with our families, that we can be fully and truly ourselves. For a few moments, we can forget our burdens and blend in with a group who calls us by our familiar names without a hint of artifice or awkwardness. This is a blessing. I find it alarming when I hear of priests who do not like priests or who do not regularly gather in their company. There is always a small percentage of priests who do not attend priestly gatherings. This does not bode well for them or their ministries.

Another asceticism is the celibate life itself. Celibacy takes on a unique challenge when it is lived among the people. Some have suggested that celibacy is only appropriate in a religious order. It is true that a religious community offers special supports for a celibate life and is clearly ordered to such a commitment. The priest in public ministry who lives in a rectory does not enjoy the support of a religious community per se. In addition, he is surrounded by people who do not share his call to celibacy. Many of them do not understand or even support it. This can be particularly isolating and a constant challenge.

However, living among the people makes our celibate witness and our commitment to God all the more visible to the people of God. Given our sex-obsessed, materialistic, and narcissistic culture, this witness of dedication and sexual self-discipline is desperately needed. The celibate priest witnesses to the immediate presence of God and to a celibate form of loving which is a rich source of grace for both the community and for himself. But it is difficult.

There is in our modern Western society a presumption of a life of comfort and entitlement. It is no accident that vocations to a dedicated life that includes significant self-denial are seen as unrealistic and, on the surface, unattractive to many. Given years of societal affluence, people now come to expect their lives to be comfortable and believe that they are entitled to have the possessions that commercials and advertisements offer. When suffering strikes, as it inevitably does to all, or their lives do not live up to the materialistic standards as advertised, which they cannot, our people often feel hurt and angry. Their hearts shout out, "Whose fault is it? Whom should I blame? Whom do I sue?"

But we have forgotten the Book of Genesis. It is the curse of humanity to live a life that includes sweat, toil, and pain. "I will intensify the pangs of your childbearing; in pain shall you bring forth children. . . . By the sweat of your face shall you get bread to eat" (Gn 3:16,19). Suffering and pain are the lot of every human life, even in wealthy societies. This is true of our lives as well. At times, we priests suffer and may even question our vocations. Sometimes priests will see the presence of hardships as a sign that they are not being good priests. "What have I done wrong?" they wonder. Does this suffering mean that we have necessarily done something wrong? No. Suffering is a part of every life: married, single, and celibate. Questions arising about our vocation can be an invitation to move even deeper into this life and commitment. Most of all, we priests ought to take comfort and strength from the life of Jesus, who was a suffering servant.

Our society has become inured with possessions and false notions; it has become entitled and narcissistic. It is in the midst of this narcissism that the priest's life is meant to be a sign of contradiction. He is to be *in the world, but not of the world.* Imbued with the spirit and grace of the gospels, the priest lives among the people, yet he is not so filled with secular values as to become salt gone flat (cf. Mt 5:13). If he purchases every electronic gadget, buys the best of everything, and lives a privileged life, he becomes more akin to a comfortable bachelor. We ought to step back regularly and observe our lives, sometimes with the help of a spiritual director or priest support group, to discern if the manner of our living is an outward witness to the gospels. For example, it is not in keeping with our calling to be seen in seedy taverns, "pickup" locations, or gay bars. Sadly, a few of our number frequent such locations.

This being *in the world but not of the world* is one of the great challenges of the diocesan priest or any priest ministering among the people. We are to affirm whatever in the people's lives and values are true signs of the Spirit at work, and of these, there are many. But we are also to be a sign of contradiction when the culture of death, entitlement, and injustice rears its ugly head. Of these, there are also many.

Because of the challenges and difficulties a priest faces, a danger will be to fall into extended periods of self-pity. It should be immediately noted that feelings of self-pity are often the doorway to behaviors that are incongruous with any Christian life, particularly that of priesthood. How many priests I have known who justified scandalous and sinful behavior with the thought that "I deserve it because of what I have given up," or "I need it to continue this difficult ministry." Instead of aiding his life, such behavior only adds to his problems. He has created yet another problem with which he has to deal. Thoughts and behaviors justifying these actions indicate salt gone flat and a soul that has fallen into the very narcissism it was meant to convert.

While the life and struggles of the priest are truly challenging, a challenge that is worthy of the most generous of souls, we should beware of a kind of "terminal uniqueness." Each of us knows some married people. Marriage is no panacea for the challenges of our celibate priests. Looking more closely at marriage, we can see that this, too, is a life of challenge and struggle. Like priesthood, it has its joys and rewards, but it also has its share of heartaches and sorrows. Exchanging a celibate priesthood for a married life might solve some of its difficulties, but it will introduce a whole new set of challenges. Before we decide to abandon our priestly commitment to enter into marriage, we would do well to speak to those who are married and inquire discreetly about their lives. From a distance, "the grass looks greener," but the reality is sobering.

Human life is challenging. It requires self-sacrifice and hard work, regardless of the vocation to which one is called. Priesthood is particularly difficult. Jesus promised us that it would be so. If we are truly followers of his, he promised, "My cup you will indeed drink" (Mt 20:23). Make no mistake about it, the more closely we follow Christ, the more we participate in his suffering and death. It is currently not in vogue to speak of the priest as sacrificial lamb or victim, but such language might help to give words to the experiences of priests today. How else can we make sense of the persistent, subliminal denigration of gospel values that daily challenges the souls of our priests?

If you have been a priest for many years and you look back at decades of service and, after reviewing your ministry, cannot find one time when your preaching, ministry, or personal witness met with disapproval, you have to ask yourself if you really preached the Gospel. If our words and homilies have never been rejected by some people and if we have never been criticized for our public stance, then we have never fully preached the message of Jesus. Jesus insisted, "Whoever wishes to come after me must . . . take up his cross, and follow me" (Mt 16:24). It was an invitation and a promise. It would not be inappropriate to see the sufferings of priesthood these past few years, especially during the crisis, as a participation in this suffering. Whether deserved or undeserved, personally culpable or not, our priesthood is a sharing in the priestly cross of Jesus. It is this cross that will purify us of our own weaknesses and sins, and it is this cross that will likewise be a sign of hope for the people who suffer greatly.

Priesthood is a difficult life. Make no mistake about it. Each of us ought to be grateful to the priests who have gone before us and have paved the way with their own faith and sacrifice. Our sacrifice is no less assured and no less important. The life of a priest is a worthy challenge and ought to be presented in this way to noble souls in search of just such a calling.

To my brother priests currently on the road up Calvary, take courage. Your sacrifice is part of your conformity to Jesus' life, and a necessary part of living your life with integrity. March on. . . .

chapter 2

A Work of Ultimate Concern

My beloved son . . . be strong lest prosperity lift you up too much or adversity cast you down.[3]

✣ St. Stephen of Hungary

JUST AS PRIESTHOOD IS MORE DIFFICULT THAN MOST OF US thought it would be, it is also a lot better. In the end, there can be no mediocrity in this life, no room for a half-hearted priesthood. It demands a personal, total, and radical commitment. I believe that one of the many learnings from the 2002 church crisis in the U.S. is that we are called to a life of full integrity and to a level of holiness that we might not have thought possible. In fact, it is the laity who has challenged us to these heights of sanctity. The people expect us to be chaste, humble, and totally dedicated servants of God. In our hearts, I suspect this is what we want for ourselves too.

This is one of the reasons that celibacy is part of the priestly commitment. As Saint Paul tells us, "An unmarried man is anxious about the things of the Lord, how he may please the Lord. But a married man is anxious about the things of the world, how he may please his wife, and he is divided" (1 Cor 7:32–34). This radical, total commitment to the "things of the Lord" is our life's calling.

But even on this side of heaven, the difficulty of its sacrifices and sorrows are strongly overshadowed by its joys and its rewards. Jesus promised that we would receive one hundredfold in this life and we priests know it is true. I cannot think of a more meaningful life. What could be more satisfying than helping people in their sorrows, giving them hope, and being an instrument of

God's grace? In the survey I conducted, mentioned in the last chapter, when asked if they believed their lives and ministries as priests make a difference in the world, 89.1 percent of the priests said yes. If young people had an inkling of the satisfaction and a taste of the joys of priestly life, many more would be knocking on rectory doors to join our ranks.

In my survey, the priests were given a statement, "Overall, I am happy as a priest." The percentage of the priests who either agreed or strongly agreed that they were happy as priests was 90.5. Only 6.2 percent indicated they were thinking of leaving the priesthood and when asked if they would do it all over again, 82.5 percent said yes. These are very strong survey results. Some in our society have gotten the impression that priestly life is sad and unfulfilling. Nothing could be further from the truth.

When researching priestly satisfaction rates in previous surveys, similar very strong results have been consistent, and thus the results of my survey should not be a complete surprise. These previous studies help to confirm my findings. The 2001 NFPC study reported that only 5 percent reported they were thinking of leaving the priesthood, 88 percent said they would choose priesthood again, and 94 percent said they were currently either very or pretty happy.[4] In short, priests find great satisfaction in being priests.

I have spent some time working with seminarians. Because they are not yet priests, they often do not have a full awareness of the depth of their calling. For example, when they are in training as chaplains in hospitals, they often see themselves as secondary and inferior to the doctors, nurses, and other health care professionals. It is true that these professionals have a noble calling and they themselves participate in the healing work of Christ. But the chaplain carries a message and a grace that is of first importance. I tell the seminarians, "Medical science can only keep people alive for so long. The end will come for us all. You help the people to live well . . . and to die well. And you offer them something that will never end." Health care professionals' work is of great concern; it has life and death consequences. But the priest's role touches issues of ultimate concern; its consequences are now and forever.

Nothing is more important. Laboring in this field of ultimate concern is a great privilege. Perhaps this is why the priest is instantly welcomed into peoples' homes. Every priest experiences this after ordination, and I suspect many are a little surprised by it. I recall speaking to a young couple who had, two years previously, moved into the town where I was ministering. They complained that it was difficult to meet people and to be welcomed by them. I thought to myself, "I've only been here a few months and I know a lot of people and have been in their homes." The priest is a welcome friend to the people. For many Catholics, he is treated as a member of their extended family. He is a symbol of our caring, compassionate God and many people want him in their lives.

Priestly Satisfaction Is High

I find it interesting and consoling how much satisfaction priests find in their ministerial lives. Survey after survey finds the same basic results: Priests love doing pastoral ministry and find great satisfaction in it. In the 2001 NFPC study, when asked more specifically about what they found of "great importance" as a source of priestly satisfaction, 90 percent endorsed "joy of administering the sacraments and presiding over liturgy;" 80 percent endorsed "satisfaction of preaching the Word;" and 67 percent endorsed "opportunity to work with many people and be a part of their lives."[5] In my own 2003–2005 survey, 92.1 percent of the priests endorsed the statement, "Overall, I feel fulfilled ministering as a priest." When given the statement, "I am committed to the ministry of the Catholic Church," the response was almost unanimous: 95.9 percent said yes.

These are incredibly high rates of commitment and satisfaction. I am confident that these rates would match up favorably with any work one might consider. In fact, in a 2003 CNN poll of five-thousand Americans only 62.9 percent said they were "happy with their current job."[6] When the priests in my survey were asked the same basic question, "Are you happy in your current ministry?" 89.8 percent of the priests agreed. Perhaps one of the most needed vocational tools is to get the word out about how happy and satisfied our priests are, perhaps having young people observe these happy priests' lives so they can see it for themselves.

People Love and Support Their Priests

People respond to their priests with gratitude. In the midst of the 2002 church crisis, Catholics in Boston, the epicenter of the ecclesial shockwave, were asked by the staff of the *Boston Globe* if they were dissatisfied with their parish priests. Only 4 percent said that they were.[7] In the midst of this crisis in the Church, 96 percent of the people supported and were satisfied with their parish priests. The people are grateful for their priests and, when given a chance, willingly show their affection.

I recall a priest who decided to leave the parish where he had been ministering for a number of years. He did not believe that the people really cared about or supported him and he became dissatisfied. So, he quietly told the bishop he wanted to be transferred and was given a new assignment. Before he left, he had the customary departure Mass and social. The priest was stunned by the outpouring of sentiment and the expressions of sorrow at his departure. He said, "If I had known how much they loved me, I would have stayed!" Like us, the laity are busy, often preoccupied, and do not always express their gratitude. But try to take away a beloved priest and the people of the parish will rise up in protest!

We priests often miss the many signs of support and appreciation that come our way. We tend to focus on the negative. The truth is that the people are regularly and in many ways expressing to us their affirmation. Sadly, we tend to tune out the positive and only let in the negative. For example, if ninety-nine people tell you after Mass how much they loved your homily, and one person criticizes it, whom do you think about at night? Many times it is our own inability to take in the warmth coming our way that results in our feeling unappreciated.

I encourage every priest to take a quiet moment and reflect upon the events of the past week. No doubt there will be a few moments of conflict and unhappiness, as there are in any life. But woven throughout the days are many words of thanks and appreciation, signs of gratitude and support, such as the hospital patient who smiles at the priest when he arrives, the parishioner who makes a special effort to shake the priest's hand after Mass on Sunday, or the grateful eyes of a person whom the pastor took a moment to call on when hearing of a death in the family. The vast majority of the people are very grateful for our presence. A key to living our priestly life with grace is to take in these moments and let the laity support us, just as much as we take in the daily conflicts and problems that agitate us so.

A Sacramental Life

Much of the priest's work is presiding at the sacraments. He is uniquely the presider at Eucharist, the sacrament of Reconciliation, and the Anointing of the Sick. He also regularly presides at baptisms, funerals, and weddings. These can become a bit routine, and at times a burden, particularly if the priest has three or more in a single day. More of us will do so in the future as our numbers dwindle and the demands keep rising.

We will have to do some realistic planning about this for the future. The plain fact is that we are going to have many fewer priests in the developed Western nations in the near future and a lot more of the faithful who need our ministry. We will have to use our priests wisely, and they will need to plan the use of their energies and time with care and thoughtfulness. We will want to ask ourselves such basic questions as, "Who is most in need of a priest's ministry? How can I best serve the people of this place?" We will also need to ask, "What is the charism of the priest in active ministry?"

Some have decried the reduced numbers of priests in this country as a negative sign for the Church. I think it is indeed a negative sign of our affluence and the materialistic narcissism of our day. The vocation "crisis" is only a crisis in the wealthier nations of the world. In fact, the Vatican reported that there is a boom in vocations internationally; in 1978 there were 63,882 major seminarians in the world and in 2001 there were 112,982. According to the secretary of the Congregation for the Clergy, "Never in the history of the Church have we had so many seminarians studying philosophy and theology."[8] Vocations go down in areas as affluence rises. Jesus had something to say about the rich and the kingdom of God.

At the same time, the calling to be a priest has been, and will always be, somewhat rare. Sadly, the world has never had enough, at least from a human perspective. Unfortunately, there have always been, and always will be, areas of the world that do not have Sunday Eucharist available. As grace-filled as the life is, it takes a heart that cares deeply for the eternal in others, eyes to see the marvels of our gracious God, and a willingness to offer one's life in service. May God grant more people this priestly heart.

Some people have suggested that the priests themselves are not supporting vocations in the United States. My 2003–2005 survey results suggest otherwise. When given the rather personal statement, "If I had a nephew, I would encourage him to become a priest," 72.7 percent of the priest sample agreed. Moreover, 72.8 percent of the priests said they actively encourage people to become priests. In surveys done by the U.S. Conference of Catholic Bishops (USCCB), 78 percent of the newly ordained acknowledge that before they entered the seminary a priest had directly asked them to consider priesthood. This direct encouragement of vocations by priests is clearly an important vocational tool. It is also a strong sign of priestly satisfaction. People who are negative about their vocations are unlikely to encourage others to follow in their footsteps.

While the priest's ministry has always been intimately connected with the sacraments, it will be even more so in the future. It will be important that our priests not become solely providers of sacraments to the exclusion of all else. Spending time with the people in a variety of settings, outside of the sacraments, is not a luxury. It is essential for the people and it is an integral part of his priestly vocation. Nevertheless, the sacraments have been and always will be a central part of his life.

Despite what is sometimes the routine of the sacraments, it is essential that the priest see in these moments a unique conferring of God's grace. Some time ago, there was a theology going around which suggested that the sacraments were merely signs that depicted what had already taken place between the individual and God. This has never been the teaching of the Church and it voids the sacraments of their real power. They are indeed signs, but within the sign is a grace-filled moment in which there is a direct transmission of God's life.

If the priest loses this sense, he loses the true life-giving force that is the Church, and his own life becomes void of much of its power as well. The Catholic Church is founded by Christ who dwells within this Church in a full and direct way. Thus the Church is a sacrament, in and of itself. That is, the Church is a sign of God's presence on this earth and this sign is itself an instrument of God's grace. Similarly, the priest is a kind of sacrament himself. His presence, as one who is *in persona Christi capitis*, is a grace for the people, despite his very human failings. As he presides at the sacraments, these unique gifts of God make holy important moments in people's lives, such as births, sickness, weddings, and funerals.

I believe that there is a kind of *reflected grace* that the priest participates in when he celebrates the sacraments. We are all aware that the priest is an instrument of God's grace in the sacraments. We know that the individuals who receive the sacraments are uniquely blessed at that moment. But priests consistently cite the sacraments as important moments in their own spiritual journeys. They speak of their presiding at the sacraments as graced moments for themselves. For example, each priest has felt at times the consoling presence of our merciful God in the confessional. All of us have sometimes experienced a sense of nourishment and a profound peace when presiding at the Eucharist. When anointing the sick, we ourselves have sometimes felt touched by God's healing grace. It seems that the priest is not only one who dispenses God's grace, but also one who receives a blessing of grace at the same time; a kind of *reflected grace* comes back to him.

I remember one of my first pastors when I was newly ordained. One day he was sick and I offered to celebrate the morning Mass in his place. He told me that he appreciated the thought but said that he wanted to do this not only for the people but also for himself. Being one whose life is closely connected to the sacraments means that the priest is intimately connected to that which is holy. He, too, is graced when he presides at the sacraments. His life becomes touched and slowly transformed by these graced moments.

I personally find it a blessing to spend time in the church and, in particular, time before the Blessed Sacrament in prayer. While God is present everywhere, God is uniquely and powerfully most present in the Eucharist. Being at home in God's house is a wonderful privilege given to the priest. God shares his house with all, but especially with the priest who is uniquely at home in this place and with him.

Fed by Grace

The priest's life then is one that is directly and intimately connected to sacred things, that is, things that are dedicated to God. He himself is dedicated to God as well. So, in a certain sense, he becomes like the church building, that is, sacred because it is dedicated to God. An apt metaphor for the priest is the chalice. When you really think of what most chalices are, they are ordinary metal underneath. The metal is hammered into shape and then dressed up with beautiful decorations, but it is still rough metal underneath. It is then totally consecrated to God's service; it ought not to be used for secular purposes.

We priests are human beings, no better and no worse than our lay brothers and sisters. But we are initially formed through the seminary and undergo a lifelong formation; we are "hammered" into shape. We are dressed up in special garments to signify the priesthood, such as the stole and the chasuble. Then, we are consecrated solely to God's service. This is one notion that helps to understand the commitment to celibacy; we are committed completely to God.

The air that the priest is meant to breathe is filled increasingly with grace. Down through his years of priestly service, he becomes more and more attuned to the ways of God. What a joy it is to see the hand of God working in people's lives! It is a special privilege to have a small part to play in these divine works. This, then, is a great blessing and joy of the priestly life. Our lives are dedicated completely to God, and to the people. Thus, they are sacred, despite our perpetually nagging human frailty.

In designated moments which we call sacraments, we are uniquely conduits of this grace. And it is not uncommon that we ourselves would witness and receive some of the power of such grace. Like every other priest, I have been moved time and again by powerful moments in the confessional. Many penitents have wept and, with them, my heart, too, has been touched. Similarly, at times our hearts are raised up in a joy-filled consolation when we offer back to the Father the body and blood of Christ on the altar. How many hearts have been consoled as we touch them in their final illness with the holy oils and dispense the last rites before they return to God? We are recipients of a *reflected grace*.

There are many trials and struggles of our priestly lives, difficulties that come from the life itself and difficulties that arise from our own broken humanity. But these are nothing compared to the majesty of our calling. The priest's life "swims" in grace. He is a friend to all that is holy and of God. To live this life with integrity and peace, he must develop the eyes to see God's work and a heart deep enough and open enough to take in these daily graces.

The people know he is a man of God. This is why they open their homes to him. Unless he betrays their trust, he is given a key to their homes and their hearts that no one else is given. They tell him their most intimate secrets, their hopes and their fears, their joys and their sins. They speak to him in the hope that, by opening their hearts to him, they have opened their hearts to God. And indeed, they have.

It is an awesome grace and responsibility, but we ought to have no fear. The grace and the power are imbedded in the sacrament of orders. In the end, this is God's work, not ours. We only have to give God the room to work . . . by giving him our all.

chapter 3

Men of Prayer

You breathed your fragrance on me; I drew in breath and now I pant for you. I have tasted you; now I hunger and thirst for more. You touched me, and I burned for your peace.[9]

✠ St. Augustine

Go before the tabernacle to establish with Jesus a simple and daily rapport of life. With the same naturalness with which you seek out a friend . . . in that same way go before the tabernacle to seek out Jesus. Make of Jesus your dearest friend, the most trusted person, the most desired and the most loved.[10]

✠ To The Priests,
Our Lady's Beloved Sons

JESUS' DISCIPLES PLEADED WITH HIM: "TEACH US HOW TO pray" (cf. Lk 11:1–4). Jesus responds with that most profound of prayers, the Our Father. Just as Jesus taught his disciples how to pray, so must we, who continue the life and work of Jesus, teach our people how to pray. It is a perennial concern and hope of theirs. They want to learn to pray.

If we are to teach them how to pray, it presumes, of course, that we priests are men of prayer. People expect us to be so. I believe that we, too, expect ourselves to be so. Sadly, this is sometimes not the case; sometimes we are not really men of prayer.

In the secular world around us, action is preferred to contemplation and working is preferred to a meditative rest. The Mary of the scriptures who sat at the feet of Jesus has been completely overshadowed by the Martha who is concerned and busy about many things. It is no wonder that we have bred a society of workaholics. Are we happier because of it? Certainly not. There is more anger, frustration, and unhappiness in our very materially wealthy society than ever before.

Unfortunately, this obsession with work to the exclusion of a healthy rest and contemplation has infiltrated and infected our priesthood. I was interviewing a priest whose life had fallen apart. We were looking at options on how best to regenerate his priesthood. Finally, I asked him, "Do you pray?" With a tone of scorn in his voice he snapped, "I don't have time to pray." I spontaneously responded, "Then you don't have time to be a priest."

In my 2003–2005 survey of priests, they were asked about their spiritual practices. A solid 80.2 percent said they go on an annual retreat and 88.0 percent said they personally received the sacrament of Reconciliation within the past year. But when asked if they pray privately more than 30 minutes per day, only 45.3 percent said yes. Frankly, I found this to be disappointing. We are men of God with an important role of teaching the people how to pray. We ourselves must be nourished and fed by a daily, personal relationship with God. *Our priests are simply not praying enough.*

The 1960s notion that "My work is my prayer," while having a sliver of truth to it, is functionally vacuous. Many of those who subscribed to the notion are no longer in priesthood. It is true that our ministry, when done in a prayerful spirit, has a nourishing quality to it. But it is not a substitute for personal, private prayer. Ministry, without a foundation of prayer, easily becomes social work. The priest is not primarily a social worker. He is a man of God whose life and ministry are meant to breathe forth the gospel. This means that the Holy Spirit must animate his life. In prayer, we open ourselves to the power of this Spirit.

Why Don't Priests Pray More?

It is easy to admonish priests to pray more and they dutifully acknowledge that they should. But then they do not. The dynamic is somewhat like physical exercise. We all know we should exercise more and quickly nod our heads when we are reminded of it. But we rarely take the advice and exercise more. Or, we might begin exercising with some enthusiasm but then fall right back into our old bad habits.

There are, no doubt, many reasons why we do not pray more. It was already noted that our priests are infected with the obsessive activism of our culture. They measure themselves by the amount of work they do. And sometimes we come to believe, erroneously of course, that our working presence is indispensable. I asked one priest in trouble, "Do you take a day off?" He responded sharply, "The parish cannot function without me." "Well," I said, as he was about to enter upon an extended course of psychological treatment, "they are going to get about six months to try."

Priests are not immediately and directly reinforced for praying. The opposite is usually the case. I recall one early morning I was praying quietly in the darkened parish church before the seven o'clock Mass. A woman came up, shook me on the shoulder, and said, "I'm glad I found you and that you're not doing anything." She went on to ask me about a rather mundane administrative issue. For many people, if you are praying, you are not gainfully occupied.

Another reason some priests do not pray privately is that they are afraid of what will surface. This might sound odd, but I have had several priests say this to me when I asked about their lack of prayer: "I don't pray because I am afraid of what I will hear." When we sit quietly in private prayer, we eventually face ourselves and the living God. This can be frightening for someone who has not faced himself and is afraid of what he might find out. It is also frightening for someone who is afraid of God. Some of us, sad to say, are actually afraid of God.

I remember a religious priest who had been personally struggling for several years with addictive behaviors. At one specific point, his life took a marked turn for the better. He started to become much healthier, psychologically and spiritually, and eventually overcame his problems. When I asked him what happened to change his life, he said that he had a powerful experience of God. He had been a religious for many years but never had a direct encounter with God. Then, one afternoon he returned to his little room in the monastery and was overwhelmed with a powerful experience of God's presence. He was filled with God's peace and love. However, he was so frightened of God that he walked out of the room! He then thought better of his behavior and returned. God was still there and showered him with his healing presence. His life was never the same. But it is interesting that he initially walked out; a monk was afraid to meet the living God!

Some priests do not pray because they are afraid that the personal hurts and pains buried in their own hearts will surface. They will have to face themselves; it is no accident that the spiritual masters have said the spiritual journey begins with self-knowledge. When the mess that lies within each of our hearts surfaces, it is painful to deal with. But facing ourselves is essential for a deep inner healing. The spiritual journey cannot begin in earnest without it.

Other priests are afraid to pray because they know that God will be there. They are afraid of what God will say to them. While evaluating priests suffering from personal problems, a common theme that emerges is a distorted image of God. They intellectually know that God is loving and forgiving. Upon deeper examination, however, it is clear that they really live as if God were a harsh and demanding tyrant. Ironically, we priests give great homilies about how much God loves everyone. We all know the right things to say, but sometimes we are actually the first people who need to hear and heed our homilies.

When we sit in silent prayer, it is true that our hurts and pains will surface, but it is then that much healing can take place. Similarly, when we sit in silence and listen to God, the message we hear most often is that God loves us just the way we are. However, many are afraid of their own inner voice of self-condemnation and self-damnation, a voice they confuse with God's.

I recall a priest in difficulty who told me, "Long ago, I made a deal with God: If you don't bother me, I won't bother you." The incongruity of such a "deal" is obvious, particularly in the life of a priest. While this priest was conscious of having made this deal, there are others for whom their lives, lived in isolation from God, have become functionally the same. It is a form of deism, an old heresy. Deism posits that God created the universe and then stepped back to watch it from a distance, not getting involved. This is not Christianity. Fortunately, the priest who made the deal with God added, "God did not keep his end of the bargain and directly intervened in my life. Boy, am I glad he did!"

It is sad to note that a number of priests have an inner conviction that the good news applies to everyone else but themselves. Priests are great at preaching good news to others, but we have difficulty truly believing that the message of forgiveness and compassion applies to us too.

I have been stunned to hear a couple of priests in difficulty say, "There is no hope for me." My response is, "What part of the New Testament did you find that in?" After a hurting priest tells me his story, often filled with pain and struggle, I will say to him, "If one of your parishioners told you that story, what would you say to him or her?" At that point, he comes out with a wonderful response, full of God's mercy and compassion. I respond, "Then why don't such consoling words apply to you?"

Once priests recognize and truly take in the good news for themselves, it can be very exciting. They experience for themselves our wonderful, loving, and forgiving God. We priests can mouth words in a homily about how merciful and compassionate God is, but if we have not experienced it for ourselves, the words are hollow. In truth, if we have not become Christians ourselves and thus know that we have been loved and forgiven by God in a very direct and real way, we have little, if anything, to give to others. It was only after a powerful experience of the resurrected Jesus, confirmed and strengthened by the Holy Spirit in Pentecost, that the apostles had the courage and enthusiasm to preach the good news.

When we are touched personally by Jesus, we know for ourselves what he has been trying to tell us and we are excited by what we have been given. This is a wonderful moment. It is good news that we spontaneously want to share.

A Taste for Prayer

Probably the most significant reason why priests, or other people, do not pray more is because they have not yet developed a taste for prayer. That is, *they have not yet developed a personal taste for God.* This chapter's opening citation from Augustine's *Confessions* captures this phenomenon well. Augustine perceived God's "fragrance," that is, he personally experienced the living God. And now, he "pants" for more. No one needs to cajole a person to pray who has already tasted God.

We spend a great deal of time training our seminarians in theology. This is a good thing. We even teach them about spirituality. This, too, is important. But we typically spend a minimal amount of time teaching them to pray. We have rightly eschewed the old quasi-monastic spiritual formation for our diocesan priests. Indeed, these men are not going to be monks. But most formation programs have not yet replaced this former prayer regimen with an intensive course in prayer suitable for their vocations. Gathering for the Liturgy of the Hours in common is important, but much more is needed.

Fortunately, many of our new young seminarians have had intense spiritual experiences that have contributed directly to their recognizing a priestly vocation. In a 2000 survey of priests ordained within the past eight years, 66 percent of diocesan priests and 64 percent of religious priests confirm that they had "an experience of spiritual awakening in [their] youth or adult years" and it was "important for [their] vocation."[11] It seems that God is reaching out—personally, directly and powerfully—and calling them to priesthood.

We will need to build on these initial religious experiences and fervor in order to develop solid men of prayer. These experiences are only the beginning. Once the initial "glow" has subsided, the real earnest work of prayer must begin. There is no other way to learn how to pray than diving in and praying. Of course, we need some guidance. But prayer is something that is best learned in the very act of praying.

As we grow into a deeper maturity in prayer, the priest will develop a familiarity with God, a kind of relaxed friendship. Saint Teresa of Avila is a fine guide in this. She spoke of becoming friends with God and about prayer as a conversation between friends. When we come to this familiarity with God, we naturally lose any neurotic fear of God while maintaining a holy fear of his awesome power.

In such conversations we do not always expect to receive sensible consolations. Rather, merely being in the presence of God brings a sense of inner peace. What happens in the soul of the friends of God who regularly immerse themselves in prayer is hard to describe. Certainly the words "peace," "rest," and a "quiet joy" come to mind. The spirit expands and the eyes seem filled with light. Rather than fearing such divine encounters, we welcome them with delight.

Beginning to Pray

There is no one right method of prayer. This is where a spiritual director can be helpful because the form a priest's prayer will take depends on his temperament, ministerial situation, the state of his spiritual life, and his time of life. The prayer forms that we use change throughout the day, the month, and throughout the seasons of our lives.

A helpful way to begin with someone, including a priest, who does not know how to pray is to suggest that the individual sit in a sacred place, such as a church, and honestly share one's inner feelings and thoughts with God. If you are happy, tell God what is making you happy; if sad, share your sorrow. In other words, tell God exactly what you would tell your closest friend. Thus, you have treated God as your closest friend, which indeed God should be. While God already knows our innermost thoughts and feelings, the act of sharing develops trust and openness to God. It opens the heart to God and this openness allows divine grace to pour in.

It is particularly important to share one's "negative" emotions with God, emotions such as anger, frustration, fear, and shame. Sometimes people erroneously think that we should only speak to God of positive things and positive emotions. They then bury the negative ones. Hiding one's negative emotions not only destroys a friendship with others, it destroys our friendship with God. In time, all that is left is a superficial smile that covers over what is really happening in the person's heart. We have a wonderful role model in Saint Teresa of Avila who said to God, "If this is how you treat your friends, it is no wonder you have so few!" She was not loath to express her anger to God.

I often tell the story of a priest I knew who was dying of AIDS. As he was nearing the end, I asked him about his prayer life. He said he had stopped praying several months ago. I was a bit surprised and asked him why. He said, "I prayed and prayed and nothing happened, so I stopped praying." When I asked him how he prayed, he said, "I sat in the chapel and gave thanks and praise to God, but nothing happened." I then asked, "Well, how are you really feeling?" He responded sharply, "I am ANGRY! I am dying of AIDS!" I suggested that he go back into the chapel and tell God exactly how he felt. The priest expressed his reticence; he was afraid to make God angry at this point in his life. But he consented and opened his heart to God, expressing the anger that had been piling up and poisoning his heart. Then, his prayer life began to move again. A short time later he died in much peace, after a powerful experience of how much God loved him just as he was.

Praying the Scriptures

The priest should have a special love of the sacred scriptures and pray them daily. If he is to be for the people a unique presence of Jesus, he must take on the mind and heart of Christ. The holy scriptures are an essential and foundational part of this presence. They embody the living heart and mind of Jesus. The priest ought to have a daily dose of this living word of God.

The lectionary of readings for the Mass are typically the daily scriptural fare of the priest in ministry; they are to him what *lectio divina* is to the monk. In his preparation for daily Mass and a brief daily homily, he will sit and "chew" on the readings for the day. He will want to reflect on how the readings resonate in his own life and in the life of his community. Consulting the writings of scripture scholars and doing a few moments of research on the texts is always helpful and recommended. Biblical commentaries are fine sources in this regard. But the critical piece is that the priest daily "ingest" the word of God. He is constantly assaulted with the values of our secular society, some good, many not so good. If he is not to be salt gone flat, he will need to counter these influences with daily doses of the heart and mind of Christ.

One of the particular ways in which the priest meditates and prays the holy scriptures is through his faithful, daily recitation of the official prayer of the Church, the Liturgy of the Hours. In the aforementioned survey, the priests were asked how regularly they pray the Liturgy of the Hours. Sad to say, only 52.8 percent said they pray all or most of it daily. This is unfortunate. Once again, it is likely that many priests do not pray the Liturgy of the Hours because they have not yet personally experienced the power and the grace of this prayer. If they did, they would be loath to skip even one of the hours. But many excuse themselves from the Office saying that they are too busy, or that the prayer form does nothing for them, or that the Office is only meaningful when done in community.

The Liturgy of the Hours carries a special efficacy. When the priest prays the hours, he joins in the official prayer of the Body of Christ and he becomes the Church praying. More than an obligation, it is a privilege and a grace. But this awareness does not begin overnight. For me, it took ten years of recitation before I could begin to "taste" the nourishment and become consciously aware of its grace. I think that many priests do not give the Liturgy of the Hours a chance. It might take many years. Don't give up!

By daily chewing on the word of God, in meditation and prayer including the Liturgy of the Hours, and by his own daily reception of the body and blood of Christ, the faithful priest will be slowly transformed. He will take on the heart and mind of Christ and, in fact, will truly become a living presence of Christ. He will be able to say with Saint Paul, "Yet I live, no longer I, but Christ lives in me" (Gal 2:20).

A Daily Hour of Prayer

I particularly recommend a daily holy hour, that is, spending one hour each day in front of the Blessed Sacrament. This was the well-known recommendation of Archbishop Fulton Sheen. I have found it invaluable. If a priest finds he cannot do one hour at a sitting, two half hours would certainly be acceptable. In the beginning, it might be a bit daunting to try to do a holy hour. For some it is best to begin with a solid 20 to 30 minutes of private prayer each day. But eventually, he will want to work up to a lengthier daily prayer, combined to yield a daily hour.

Priests sometimes ask me what they should do during this hour. We return to the basic notion that we ought to use whatever kind of prayer that works the best for us. Some will use a prayerful recitation of the Liturgy of the

Hours. Others will engage in a silent meditation or pray the rosary. Some will open their hearts to God and express their deepest feelings and concerns. Still others will meditate directly on the word of God. I use a combination of these prayer forms, as many people do. The key is to remain present to the Lord for an extended period of time.

I know that many, perhaps most, priests who read this recommendation will immediately think, "This is a nice idea but I don't have time for a daily holy hour. There is too much to do." I respond by making you a promise. *I promise you that if you do a daily holy hour, your life will accomplish more, not less.* Your ministries will be more fruitful, even a busy parish ministry. The truth of this promise resonates in our hearts. God is the source and animator of our lives and priesthood. It is he who makes them fruitful. To engage in this daily hour of prayer places our ministries directly in God's hands. It is an act of faith. Trust in God. Try it.

Concluding Remarks

The priest who does not pray privately and does not feed on the word of God will find that the fruits of his labors will be limited and that his ministry will lack sufficient depth. He will be more prone to personal problems as well. His house will not be the house built on rock but rather the dwelling built on sand. And surely, as it does for every life, the wind and rain will come. While I would not want to reduce every personal problem to a lack of spirituality, there is an intimate connection between them. It is no accident that there is a maxim in Alcoholics Anonymous: "Spirituality is the first thing to go and the last thing to return." When our spiritual lives suffer and begin to deteriorate, the rest of our lives are not far behind.

The ministry of prayer is a foundational work of the priest. We begin our service to the people by praying for them. The Code of Canon Law recognizes the importance of prayer when it insists that each Sunday one of the Masses said by the pastor would be "*pro populo*," for the people (Canon 534). So, too, I believe a foundational work of the bishop is to pray for the people of his diocese. It is no coincidence that people regularly say to their priests, "Father, please pray for me." It is a request that we should not take lightly or dismiss. We ought to be serious in fulfilling this noble request.

People want their priests to be men of prayer. They want someone who is in touch with this wonderful God of ours. They want a man whose eyes and face radiate God's grace and whose heart is at peace. They want a priest who will love them and forgive them, just as God does. He can only do this if he is filled with the Spirit. He can only do this if he is a man of prayer. But this will not happen after one or two years or even five. It will be the fruit of a lifetime of prayer and faithful service. It will be such a slow and subtle change that the priest himself will not be fully aware of the wonders that God is doing in his soul.

Praying is an act of faith. It is a simple statement that God is in charge, not us. Prayer is also an important way that God fills us with his divine presence. Eventually, after many years of faithfulness to prayer, we come to know that God fills our souls with his sweet presence. As Saint Augustine knew, God touches us and we taste him. Now we hunger for God all the more. People want such men of prayer and men of God. We, ourselves, want to be such men. We begin and end this journey in prayer because our journey begins and ends with God.

chapter 4

The Priest as a Friend of God: Today's Struggle for Priestly Identity[12]

"As the Father has sent me, so I send you." And when he had said this, he breathed on them and said to them, "Receive the holy Spirit. Whose sins you forgive are forgiven them, and whose sins you retain are retained."

✢ JOHN 20:21-23

On a Sunday morning a few years ago, a newly assigned pastor arrived for the first time at his large parish. While the priest vested for the Sunday liturgy in the sacristy, the head eucharistic minister was assigning stations to the other eucharistic ministers for the distribution of communion. After the assignments to the laity were made, the man looked at the new pastor, and in a voice that all in the sacristy could hear, said, "Father, you will be giving out communion in the choir loft." He added, "This is so people will see there is no difference between the priest and everyone else."

Words similar to those of this eucharistic minister have been echoed and reechoed in recent years as a kind of mantra in the Catholic Church: "There is no difference between the priest and everyone else." With such a statement often repeated, it is not surprising that some priests speak of a crisis of identity. Indeed, if the priest is no different, then it must follow that we have no unique identity.

There are many signs that such a struggle with identity has been occurring in the presbyterate. A few short years ago, at a national Catholic convention focusing on the priesthood, much of the discussion was around the rising pastoral workload and our aging, fewer priests. At the end of the plenary session, one of the priest delegates said, "I can stand more work; what I can't stand is this ambivalence about who I am." It was a stunning comment that left the room in a hushed silence. If this priest's experience is representative of the experience of the wider presbyterate, then a more pressing problem than the reduced numbers of priests and accompanying increased workload is the need to delineate and inculcate the identity of a priest. Indeed, in a recent international convention of leaders of English-speaking priest councils, the majority of the conference was dedicated to the modern challenge of priestly identity.

Another sign, I believe, of this struggle with priestly identity is a recent trend among a portion of the newly ordained priests. A significant percentage of younger priests appears to have a strong connection with external signs of the priesthood. For example, there are some who wear cassocks and birettas; a few even wear capes. Some young priests address each other in private more formally as "Father," even though they are friends. I believe that external signs of one's vocation are good and I support their use. At the same time, these behaviors of some young clerics stand out as unusual and this phenomenon deserves some thoughtful attention.

Instead of lauding or criticizing such behavior, we might first try to understand it. What does such behavior tell us about the priesthood today? One possible interpretation is that this insistence on external signs of the priesthood may be a reaction to today's lack of an inner identity of our priests. This behavior may be a largely unconscious expression of the need to discover an inner sense of who the priest is.

While the use of external signs of priesthood may facilitate this process, such signs will not be fully effective unless we priests, and the laity, are able to complement these external signs with an inner appropriation of a unique priestly identity.

Anticlericalism Following Clericalism

If the priesthood is currently suffering from identity confusion, in the minds of both priests and laity, the first step in addressing this confusion is to investigate its genesis. How did this confusion come about? Two possible causes quickly surface. . . .

First, we are in a period of anticlericalism in which the charism of the priesthood is being downplayed. I heard the renowned church historian Msgr. John Tracy Ellis say that every period of anticlericalism in church history has been preceded by a period of clericalism. Indeed, our current period of anticlericalism was preceded by a time of clericalism. For example, in the previous era, people believed that the priest was better than other people.

Because the priest was thought to be better, this led to erroneous beliefs such as the priest is immune to psychological problems and impervious to mundane human struggles. It did not occur to many people that priests could suffer from depression, anxiety, and the more distressing kinds of behavior problems. Thus, when allegations of misconduct and other psychological defects surfaced publicly, they were initially met with skepticism by some of the faithful: "How can this be?" some could be heard saying in disbelief, "He is a priest!" In the wake of allegations of priestly misconduct published in the media, the erroneous idea that priests are beyond human problems has been soundly thrashed.

Today, the danger is to go to the other extreme and to posit that priests are psychologically inferior and defective compared to the laity who "lead a more balanced life." I recently heard a number of such insinuations, both privately and in the media. The suggestion today is that a celibate, male Roman Catholic priesthood is defective and abnormal. In such a climate, it is not hard to understand how a disparaging of the priesthood would occur and a concomitant weakening of priestly identity.

Being Equal Does Not Mean Being the Same

One of the current mantras of our anticlerical period is the statement, "Priests are no different from anyone else." This is precisely the phrase uttered by the head eucharistic minister who asked the new pastor to distribute communion in the choir loft. It is clearly a reaction against a rank ordering of vocations in a previous era. The Second Vatican Council spoke of a universal call to holiness. Our society holds the equality of all peoples as a sacred value. This is good.

However, in the United States, equality is often equated with being the same. We reject discrimination in all its forms and vehemently claim that all are equal. Thus, many conclude that there is "no difference between the priest and everyone else," because we believe that all are equal and thus must be the same.

It is indeed true that God has created all people as equals. But their equality does *not* derive from their being the same. In fact, there are a plethora of differences. Some people are smarter than others; some have different skin color; and we are regularly faced with gender-based differences.

The two genders are equal, but they are not the same. Some of the psychological and theological differences are explored in Chapter Seven. Differences in gender result in different roles. For example, the physiological differences give women the exclusive role of bearing children. Theologically, the Catholic Church has said directly and consistently that ordained priesthood is a masculine role. Neither role makes one gender better than the other, but they are different.

Throughout the sacred scriptures we see evidence that some men and women were called to unique relationships with God, not because they were better than others, but simply because God chose them. For example, the prophets again and again asserted that they fulfilled a prophetic role as a unique spokesperson for God, because God himself had chosen them. Amos said, "I was no prophet . . . I was a shepherd and a dresser of sycamores. The Lord took me from following the flock, and said to me, Go, prophesy to my people Israel" (Am 7:14–15). Amos was a prophet because God chose him. So, too, God chose such great mystics as Juliana of Norwich and Catherine of Siena to be recipients of a unique mystical grace. They were given these revelations in order to share them with others. In God's eyes we are all equal, although clearly we are *not* all the same and God does *not* shed the same graces on all.

If we priests are to recover a sense of our own identity, we must eschew the mantra that priests are the same as everyone else. While we are decidedly human and thus inherently flawed because of sin, as we have been painfully reminded these past few years, the truth of the priesthood is that it is different and it carries a unique and powerful grace for the good of the People of God. Priesthood has its own identity that shapes the priest and offers a unique and necessary gift to the Church. At the same time, we must quickly add that this does not make the person of the priest better than others; but it does make us different.

A Church of Six Sacraments

There is a second trend that has helped to give rise to the current mantra, "Priests are no different from anyone else." This is the important recovering of the centrality of the sacrament of Baptism.

In the post-Vatican II era, the sacrament of Baptism has found its rightful place as central to the Christian life. It is the sacrament of Baptism that begins the life of Christ in the individual and it is upon this sacrament that the rest of the Christian life builds.

As a result, the truth of the "Priesthood of the Faithful" has been emphasized. We are all "priests" and thus called to share in the one priesthood of Jesus Christ. As a natural conclusion, the work of all the baptized has been stressed. All the faithful are called to share in the work of Jesus. As a result, there has been a necessary blossoming of lay ministries and an increasingly active involvement of the laity in the work of the Church. This is a grace for all the People of God.

However, as we have consciously emphasized the priesthood of all the faithful and their rightful place in continuing the work of Jesus, we have unwittingly de-emphasized the ordained priesthood. Some priests are floundering with understanding their rightful roles with so much of their previous work now being done by the laity. And this confusion about priesthood is as much present in the minds of the laity as it is in our priests.

The Church today seems to be a Church of six sacraments, not seven. The six sacraments are preached and taught, but the uniqueness and efficacy of the sacrament of Holy Orders are rarely mentioned. In an effort to emphasize Baptism and the universal priesthood of Jesus, the truth of the sacrament of Orders has all but vanished from our ecclesial consciousness.

I believe this understanding of the universal priesthood of Jesus is important, as is the multiplication of lay ministries. Not only does the Church need lay ministers, it is their rightful place. However, this necessary development ought not to take place at the expense of the ordained priesthood. The two need to coexist and be interrelated; both are integral to the life of the Church.

The two priesthoods, the priesthood of the faithful and the ordained priesthood are not different merely in degree. It is not that one has a bit more of priesthood than the other. Rather, they are different in kind. Both share in the priesthood of Jesus but they do so in different ways and they have different identities. They are not the same.

"Father, Pray for Me"

It is time for us to recover a proper sense of the sacrament of Orders. It is important that we rediscover the identity of the priest, not only for the sake of the priests but also for the good of the entire Church. We must state clearly that, although we priests are not better, our charism is decidedly different. And it behooves us to begin to delineate what some of these differences might be. The question arises, "Where might we begin to look for this unique priestly identity?"

One place to begin the search is in a simple experience that every priest has day after day. A member of the laity will say to us with a sincere and earnest heart, "Father, please pray for me." If one subscribes to the mantra, "The priest is no different," then the request is meaningless. In that case, the priest might justly respond, "What good are my prayers? Go, pray for yourself." I have heard of priests giving such an insensitive response. But, day after day, week after week, in parishes, schools, and hospitals throughout the world, priests are beseeched to pray for a myriad of people's intentions. Why would so many of the laity ask for our prayers?

Is it because we are thought to be holier? It may be that some still believe the priest is necessarily holier and thus this would be the dying remnant of an earlier clerical era. But, I think that the reality is much more profound and rightfully enduring.

The truth is that the people of God believe and expect the priest to have a unique relationship with God. I believe that they expect the priest to be part of an "inner circle," or a kind of "friend of God." In Roman times there was a group known as "Friends of Caesar." Pontius Pilate appeared to have had the distinction of belonging to this group (Jn 19:12). In early imperial times a friend of the emperor was often someone who was the emperor's official representative.[13] Presumably, such friends had a unique access to this important person. In a similar way, the faithful expect their priests to be official representatives, or a special "Friend of God."

When the faithful are in need and desperate for God's ear, they will beseech a priest and others to intercede for them with God. The Catholic Church, while exhorting all to have a direct and personal relationship with God, has encouraged the use of intermediaries. We regularly implore the assistance of the Blessed Virgin as well as our favorite saints. While it is rarely mentioned publicly, many of the faithful pray to their deceased mothers and fathers and other loved ones for their intercession and help. It is natural and, I think, a good practice of the faithful. While we are all to nurture a close and personal relationship with God, our religion is not simply an individual and vertical one; the role of the community and spiritual leaders is important. We should often ask for others' help, particularly those who might be of unique assistance.

As noted in the previous chapter, a foundational role of the priest is to pray for the people. If God is the source of all grace and blessing, and if the priest is called to be a "Friend of God," then an integral part of his ministry is to intercede with God on behalf of the people.

Archbishop Timothy Dolan, in his excellent work *Priests for the Third Millennium*, related a story from his early days of priesthood which illustrates this truth. He was called to the hospital to visit a man in his 60s who was about to undergo a life-threatening surgery. The man assigned tasks to each of his sons present in the hospital room. One was to go over the man's will; another was to take care of business arrangements; a third was assigned the task of caring for the man's wife. At that point, Father Dolan asked, "And what am I to do?" The response was swift and insightful, "Immediately twelve eyes glared at me, all surprised that I had even asked such a question and . . . the father, quickly responded, 'Why, Father, you pray, of course!'—as all the sons nodded in agreement, astonished that I had even to ask."[14]

I am personally convinced of the primary importance of our ministry of prayer and each morning I begin the day by praying for the people whom I serve, particularly in that most efficacious prayer, the Eucharist. It is my most important work. It is what the people of God most often ask me to do for them. They say, day after day, "Father, please pray for me."

The Presence of a Priest as Grace

I recall making the point to a group of priests at their annual convocation that we priests are called to have a unique friendship with God. At that point, in front of the entire assembled presbyterate, a priest complained, "Are you saying that a priest is better than other people?" Again, we see a variation of the modern mantra surface: "Priests are no different from anyone else."

How could one respond to such a challenge? The thought came, which I shared with those gathered, that the scriptures give us a clear model in this regard. Jesus loved everyone and called everyone to salvation. However, there were twelve men with whom he had a particularly close relationship. He called them to have a unique friendship with him that others did not enjoy. For three years, he walked with them, ate with them, and spoke to them plainly and not in parables. They were not chosen because they were better than others. In fact, we do not know why he picked them over others, and the scriptures are embarrassingly clear about the apostles' flaws, but they were his choice. Jesus offered to them a kind of intimate friendship that he did not offer to others.

It is no different today. We priests are not better, but we are called by Jesus to have a unique friendship with him and thus a unique friendship with God. The people expect such a friendship and, truth to tell, we priests hope to have such a relationship as well. We earnestly desire to be friends of God.

It is no accident, then, that much of what a priest does in the course of his ministry is simply showing up. He is invited to receptions, ball games, dinner parties, and picnics. He spends his days visiting the sick and the homebound, the schools, and the nursing homes. He offers words of consolation; he administers the sacraments; but first and of critical importance, he shows up. Because of his presence, the faithful feel blessed.

It should be added that, in these days of rising demands on the priesthood and fewer numbers, priests will necessarily show up at fewer gatherings. It would be problematic for a priest to measure his effectiveness by how many functions he attends, a not uncommon tendency. Rather, his mere presence in the parish is showing up and he will likely find that attending a few well-selected events is more efficacious than a frenetic calendar of activity.

The faithful see the presence of a priest among them as a source of grace. Their confidence in us should embolden us to lay our hands on the faithful when they are sick and pray for their healing. Their confidence should inspire us to pray with them. We should not be reticent to say in public the time-honored phrase, "May God bless you."

The priest is a kind of sacrament with a small "s." As a friend of God and official representative, ordained by the Church, we represent what is sacred and are meant to be a conduit of grace, often in ways that we do not even recognize. While consciously aware of our very human faults and limitations, the presence of the priest is to be a source of grace for the community to which we are sent. This truth is easily obscured by excessive activity and overwork on the part of our priests today, a significant danger. If priests feel that they must constantly be working and implementing programs, then it is likely they are missing a deeper truth: God is the source of all grace and our most important work is to let him shine through us. We should often beseech his blessing on ourselves and on all the people. We must first fulfill our calling to be "Friends of God." The scriptures remind us that the twelve initially spent three years with Jesus before they engaged in their public ministry.

Aspects of Friendship with God

The priest might rightly ask, "What does this friendship with God mean for me? Is there a model for such a friendship?" The nature of such a friendship is best seen in the lives of the apostles. I offer the following as six aspects of this friendship:

1. As noted previously, a friendship with God follows only upon acceptance of the divine initiative. *It is God who chooses* and God does not reveal the reason for the choice. It is simply a mysterious, divine prerogative. "It was not you who chose me, but I who chose you" (Jn 15:16).
2. *The apostles leave everything to follow Jesus.* Our God is a "jealous God" (Ex 20:5). The price of this friendship is a complete self-surrender. As noted previously, such a demand makes the practice of clerical celibacy more understandable. While some point out that the apostle Peter was married, the scriptures give the clear impression that he left all behind to follow Jesus.[15] We are to be like the person finding the buried treasure in the field; he gave up everything for this treasure. The scriptures note that he did so with "joy" (Mt 13:44). We, too, should be full of joy in the divine treasure for which we have sacrificed everything.
3. Jesus speaks to his friends "plainly." As the scriptures tell us, "And when he was alone, those present along with the Twelve questioned him about the parables. He answered them, 'The mystery of the kingdom of God has been granted to you. But to those outside everything comes in parables'" (Mk 4:10–11). Furthermore, Jesus tells his disciples, "I have called you friends, because I have told you everything I have heard from my Father" (Jn 15:15). It is clear that *Jesus reveals to his friends directly and plainly the living truth*

of God. The sacred deposit of faith might be best described as an ongoing, divine communication revealed to the Church.[16] The deposit of faith only lives when it is planted in the soil of a relationship or friendship with God. We ought to cherish, and never undervalue, this living gift given to God's friends. It is from this gift received, and confirmed by the Church, that the priest is then called by the Church to preach. He is the ordinary and official preacher of the Word.

4. These twelve special friends of God enjoyed a unique relationship with Jesus. They traveled with him. They were his daily companions. They ate with him. One of the disciples laid his head on Jesus' chest. They enjoyed a regular discourse with him: They had direct access to him and often asked him questions. Then, as well as today, *the friends of Jesus have an enviable familiarity with him.* Today's friends of God ought to be found often in prayer, opening their hearts and minds to this regular and familiar discourse with God.
5. *Any true friendship involves both joys and sorrows.* It is the same in a friendship with God, only more so. A divine friendship carries with it a peace that the world cannot give (Jn 14:27) and a joy that is "complete" (Jn 15:11). Its blessings are inestimable. At the same time, as noted in the first chapter, Jesus promised his disciples, "The cup that I drink, you will drink" (Mk 10:39). Any true friends of God must carry the cross of Jesus. If we have not suffered so, we cannot truly be called friends of God. Priests are acutely aware of the sufferings that today's friendship entails.
6. The friends of God continue the ministry of Jesus. While all the faithful continue the work of Jesus in some way, the priest *as a friend of God is called to engage in the ministry of Jesus directly, explicitly, and totally.* Jesus told Peter three times, "Feed my lambs" (Jn 21:15). The priest most explicitly and fully

continues the life of Christ in the Eucharist. The Eucharist and the priesthood are inseparable.

Priesthood as a Gift to the Church

In our frenetic era, priests today suffer from the increasing demand to do more and more work. Perhaps we feel compelled to give in to these unrealistic demands because we have lost a sense of who we are. Now we try to plug the hole of our lost inner identity with a crushing ministerial pace. It is an unsatisfying and frustrating endeavor. No amount of external signs or work can substitute for a solid inner identity.

Before the priest *does* anything, he *is* something. He is called to be a Friend of God. He is an official representative of the Church and of God. He is called to be a sign of hope. People ask him for prayers because of who he is. I believe priests instinctively come to know this truth.

Today, the priesthood is under siege from many directions. One of the reasons for this is our own sinfulness. It would not be good to underestimate the damage that our weaknesses can and have caused. Our sins can obscure our friendship with God. Indeed, we priests are often discouraged by our own sinfulness and failure. It is hard for us to reconcile our blessed calling with our human limitations. We think that true friends of God should be spiritual giants whose achievements are towering.

We ought to return to the basic truth that we are not God's friends because we are better than others or because we are spiritually advanced. Rather, we are friends because God has chosen us to be so, and *the efficacy of our friendship might be found more in our human weakness than in our spiritual gifts*. Saint Paul learned this from God who told him, "My grace is sufficient for you, for power is made perfect in weakness" (2 Cor 12:9). Human weakness is the conduit for the power of God.

It is humanly difficult to hold onto both truths simultaneously: First, we priests are sinners and no better than anyone else; second, we have been given a gift of inestimable value. This gift of priesthood is not a personal attribute that the priest wears for his personal exaltation or his own benefit; rather, it is a gift to the whole Church.

Conclusion

The rising workload and unrealistic expectations placed upon our aging, dwindling numbers of priests is a significant issue that needs to remain on the Church's agenda. But no amount of work, large or small, will be sustainable by our priests without a strong conviction in the identity and efficacy of the priesthood. Because the priesthood is a necessary gift to the entire Church, the issue of priestly identity ought to be of concern to all the People of God.

We are a Church of seven sacraments, not six. The importance of the sacrament of Baptism and the priesthood of the faithful are only strengthened, and not diminished, with a solid understanding of the sacrament of Orders and a strong presbyterate. A proper understanding of the sacrament of Orders should not lead to clericalism, but to a life of service.

The priest is different, not because of a humanity that has been elevated beyond human frailty and sinfulness, but because of an imbedded grace that shines most brightly through his weakness.

The priest is not better than others, but he is different. Together with his brother priests and his bishop, he is called to have a unique friendship with Jesus mirroring the lives of the twelve. The People of God know this. They have always and will always continue to utter that timeless request, "Father, please pray for me."

chapter 5

Self-Will Run Riot

So our troubles . . . are basically of our own making. They arise out of ourselves, and the alcoholic is an extreme example of self-will run riot. . . . We must be rid of this selfishness. We must, or it kills us! God makes that possible.

✢ Alcoholics Anonymous[17]

HUMAN BEINGS ARE ESSENTIALLY GOOD. WE WERE created in God's image. We have a built-in desire for what is good and an inner drive to seek it. However, there is also evil in the world and it has infected us. As Saint Paul wrote, "For I do not do the good I want, but I do the evil I do not want" (Rom 7:19). If human beings are given unchecked power and they are not held accountable for their actions, the results can be ugly. As the oft-quoted line from Lord Acton noted, "Power tends to corrupt and absolute power corrupts absolutely." Humans need to be held accountable for their actions. It keeps our little foibles from becoming major problems and it forces us to do our best.

There is limited accountability in the priesthood today. This is most unfortunate. Priests can get away with behavior which people in secular business would be fired for. Of course, most priests do not abuse their authority and function admirably in this current environment. But there are a few priests with problem personalities and difficulties necessarily occur. Also, even the good priests act better when held directly accountable for what they do. This suggests the need to institute more accountability structures in the priesthood than we currently have.

The lack of adequate accountability is due to a variety of structural issues. The Catholic Church rightly shies away from any approach that would promote the old problems of Trusteeism in which the laity controlled the parish and the pastor. Eventually Trusteeism bred its own scandals, conflicts, and infighting, including individual parishes schismatically breaking from their communion with the diocese, and towns rioting over which candidate they wanted as their pastor. Instead, we priests are assigned by our bishops; we are not hired by congregations. Also, the pastor has authoritative decision-making power in the parish.

I believe these aspects of our institution are good. They not only overcome the problems of Trusteeism, they also give the pastor freedom to preach the Gospel in its entirety without fear that parishioners, upset by an authentic Gospel challenge, will conspire to fire him. They also leave him and the parish largely free from ugly contests for power among factions in the parish community. Finally, this centralized, top-down authority gives stability and cohesion to a Church which is two-thousand years old and spans the entire globe. There must be a central authority with decision-making responsibility to keep such a large organization together and going in the same direction.

The downside of this arrangement is that the priest in the parish can become virtually immune to the complaints and feelings of his parishioners. If he has a personality problem, their only recourse is to complain to the bishop. But given the protections the pastor is afforded in this structure, it is difficult even for the bishop to take action without a virtual "smoking gun."

This structure is not problematic when the priest is a caring and empathetic man who is well balanced, both psychologically and spiritually, and strives to serve the people with humility. It is my experience that the majority of pastors are such fine men. We should be reminded that the large majority of parishioners are happy with their parish priests as noted in the *Boston*

Globe survey cited in Chapter Two. Recall that only 4 percent were dissatisfied with their parish priest in the Boston area, even during the intense crisis of 2002. However, a few of our priests have serious interpersonal problems and their personal foibles become exacerbated by the lack of accountability. Then, the parishioners suffer.

Even if we are not so marred, we priests all benefit from being held accountable for our behaviors. It makes even the best of us perform and behave at our very best. For ours and the Church's welfare, we need regular feedback from our superiors and from those whom we serve. Priests need to know when they are doing well and when they are not. It is in such a healthy environment of regular feedback that our pastoral skills are sharpened and our flaws are slowly healed. It's just plain good management for any organization, including a church.

Obedience Is the Antidote

There are some accountability structures already in place. First and foremost, the priest promises obedience to his bishop (or major superior if he is a member of a religious order). In *Presbyterorum Ordinis* of the Second Vatican Council, the bishop is counseled to regard the priests as his "indispensable helpers and advisers." On the priests' part, the same document said, "the very unity of [priests'] consecration and mission requires their hierarchical union with the order of bishops."[18]

Promising obedience to one's bishop is an integral part of the Rite of Ordination and we priests ought not to dismiss it. I believe it fair to say that the priest who is not obedient to his bishop, barring major and obvious malfeasance on the part of the bishop, is not being faithful to his priesthood. These are strong words, but I think they are justified.

This obedience is not the obedience of slaves, but of free men. We are not unthinking robots, but adults who interact with our bishops as mature people. For example, we are obliged to speak candidly with our bishops when we perceive that important issues are at stake and when we believe they would benefit from hearing our perspective. Similarly, we have a serious obligation to speak up when we believe that Gospel values are in danger of being compromised.

But we ought to beware of believing that we are somehow uniquely blessed to know the truth of which others are not aware. If we view ourselves and our viewpoints as superior to the ideas of all others, it may be that the rampant narcissism in our society has subtly infected us. There is much narcissism in our society and, unfortunately, there are significant traces of it in the priesthood as well.

The antidote is obedience. Exercising our priestly promise of obedience is inherently an affirmation that, as individuals, we do not know everything. It also is an affirmation of our belief that the Holy Spirit works through our Church, especially its leaders.

In this postmodern era, the place of authority has been not only questioned, it is often discounted. Postmodern deconstructionism is a philosophical approach that captures some of this modern thought. A preeminent spokesman of this philosophy, French deconstructionist Jacques Derrida, has put forth a series of ideas that promotes people becoming free from every external power. In his list of repressive authority he includes dogmatism, orthodoxy, and religious authority.

In the postmodern world, authority, at best, is suspect. At worst, it is considered to be inherently corrupt.

It appears that the media unwittingly support the postmodern deconstruction of authority by seeking to discredit just about any form of authority in our society. Discrediting authority makes especially good press. It is true that the media have an important role in holding our public authorities accountable. However, the zeal with which they take on this aspect of their role and the crusading spirit with which they go after people in authority ought to make us question their balance and fairness. In this postmodern milieu in which we live, there is a tendency for all of us, including priests, to dismiss the important role of authority in our lives.

The Gospels themselves delineate a clear line of authority. We see several statements by Jesus confirming the absolute authority of the Father, which is passed to the Son, and then to his disciples. For example, Jesus said, "All things have been handed over to me by my Father" (Mt 11:27). Jesus then gives explicit authority to his disciples, "Whoever receives you receives me, and whoever receives me receives the one who sent me" (Mt 10:40). And again, "He summoned the Twelve and gave them power and authority over all demons and to cure diseases, and he sent them to proclaim the kingdom of God" (Lk 9:1–2).

It must be quickly added that authority in the New Testament must be an authority of service and humility. "The Son of Man did not come to be served but to serve and to give his life as a ransom for many" (Mt 20:28). Just as bishops in authority ought to view their leadership as one of service, priests in subordinate roles ought to understand their mature obedience as an important virtue and charism of the priesthood.

Postcrisis Relationship of Priests and Bishops

The church crisis of 2002 in the United States appears to have had a significant deleterious effect on the relationship of bishops and priests. In my own postcrisis survey, the priests were given the statement: "The church crisis has negatively affected my view of Church leadership." A majority, 53.7 percent, agreed with the statement.

The relationship between a priest and his bishop is an important one, more than simply employer-employee. The Vatican II document *Christus Dominus* noted, "All priests, whether diocesan or religious, share and exercise with the bishop the one priesthood of Christ."[19] It is a sacred, sacramental bond.

The bishop is both father and brother to the priests. *Christus Dominus* also said bishops are to regard the priests as "sons and friends."[20] When one of these roles (e.g., father) is emphasized to the exclusion of the other (e.g., brother), then the relationship becomes distorted. If he becomes only a brother and loses a sense of his role of shepherd and leader, then he becomes ineffective. If he is only a father and a leader, and loses sight of his priests as brothers, then he becomes too distant and loses a life-giving bond necessary for his priests and for himself.

After the Dallas 2002 meeting, one bishop said privately, "One of the biggest mistakes we bishops made was to speak of 'you priests.'" This suggests that bishops had separated themselves too much from their priests and were in danger of losing a connection to them as brothers. Perhaps bishops today might reclaim more strongly the relationship of brother and friend to their priests. In this fraternal setting, the virtue of obedience to one's bishop is more inviting.

Presbyterorum Ordinis of Vatican II added that priests owe their bishops "reverence" and "sincere charity and obedience," while the bishops "are to take the greatest interest they are capable of in their (priests') welfare, both temporal and spiritual."[21] The recent survey results suggest that this obligation of looking out for the priests' welfare is perceived as being compromised. Only 27.8 percent of surveyed priests believed that "priests with allegations of abuse are being treated fairly by the Church," and less than half of the priests, 43.5 percent, believed that they would be dealt with fairly if they were accused of misconduct.

Priests today are feeling vulnerable and unsafe. They know that false allegations, while rare, do happen; and if accused, they do not think they will be treated fairly, that is, they fear that they will automatically be treated as if they are guilty. As one priest said, "I am one phone call away from the rest of my life being over." Whether this is an accurate perception or not, it is important because it threatens the sacred bond of trust between bishop and priest.

But it would be an exaggeration to believe that most priests disapprove of their own bishops. In fact, my survey suggests the opposite. When speaking about their own bishops, the priests were strongly positive. Seventy-five-point-four percent said, "I have a good relationship with my bishop"; 67.6 percent "approve of the way my bishop is leading the diocese"; and 76.7 percent agree with the statement, "Overall, I am satisfied with my bishop." In assessing approval rates for those in authority, such percentages are high. For example, the previously cited CNN poll of 5,000 adult workers reported only 43 percent were "happy with their current boss."[22] On the other hand, the strong majority of the priests profess to have a good relationship with their own bishop. They approve of and are satisfied with his leadership.

A Church Guided by the Holy Spirit

In addition to the bishop, there are other venues in which the priest exercises his charism of obedience. He is also to be obedient to the teachings of the Catholic Church. Clearly there is a hierarchy of teachings. Solemn papal pronouncements and conciliar documents are given more weight than ordinary ecclesial documents. But the priest should be loath to consider his own judgment more informed or enlightened than any Church teaching. It is true that there have been great prophetic reformers in the history of the Catholic Church who have been inspired by the Holy Spirit. However, I would venture that for every person who is truly called to a prophetic voice today, there are scores, perhaps hundreds, of misguided, would-be prophets.

There is a well-known phrase from the wisdom of the Twelve Steps of Alcoholics Anonymous: "self-will run riot." At Saint Luke Institute, a residential treatment program for clergy and religious, we use this phrase when speaking of priests or religious who are so entrenched in their own views they cannot listen to others or take in constructive feedback. They quickly discount their bishops or superiors. They also discount the words of their therapists. They reject feedback even from their own peers. In a word, they are incorrigible.

It reminds me of a story about a man on a busy highway who was telephoned by his wife. He answered his cell phone and his wife warned him about a car on the highway that was going in the wrong direction. She said she heard it on the news and wanted to alert her husband. "Frank," she said, "Watch out when you're driving. There is an idiot going the wrong way on the highway." The man replied, "Martha, I know exactly what you mean. In fact, it's not just one car going in the wrong direction. There are hundreds of them!"

Occasionally we meet someone who is going in the wrong direction and does not know it. He believes that he is right and everybody else is being misled. Sadly, some are not willing to take in any feedback and thus remain on the wrong course. If the whole Church is going in one direction and a particular priest is going in another, he ought to wonder if the problem is his.

We believe that the Catholic Church was founded by Jesus himself and is unerringly headed toward its final consummation in Christ. Jesus promised that he would not abandon us. Even now, through the power of the Holy Spirit, he infallibly guides the Church, especially through the ministry of Peter's successor and the bishops in union with him. Obedience to one's bishop and to the Holy Father not only helps to counteract our own human errors, *it is an act of faith*.

Ultimately, I believe that every priest, sometime during the course of his priesthood, will be challenged on this article of faith. Do we really believe that this is the Church founded by Jesus that is being infallibly led by the Spirit? It is a watershed moment in every priestly life. He is being challenged to learn more deeply that this Church, staffed by weak and frail human beings, is in its deepest core the Church founded by Jesus that is unerringly guided by the Holy Spirit. If we come to recognize this theological truth, we will never want to place ourselves outside the barque of Peter.

Sadly, there are some fringe groups within the Catholic Church itself whose stance seems to say, "We know what's best for the Church." They reject ecclesial authority and often even reject the direction in which the Church is headed. Some of these groups are on the theological far right and others are on the far left. Cardinal George from Chicago noted this sad trend in his remarks to John Paul II:

> The church's mission is threatened internally by divisions which paralyze her ability to act forcefully and decisively. On the left, the church's teachings . . . are publicly opposed. . . . On the right, the church's teachings might be accepted, but bishops who do not govern exactly and to the last detail in the way expected are publicly opposed. The church is an arena of ideological warfare.[23]

Ironically, in this regard, the far left and the far right are much alike, perhaps to their mutual consternation. What they have in common is a rejection of the leadership of the Church and often challenge the direction in which the Church is going. They might think of themselves as exercising a prophetic voice. It is possible. But it is more likely that they are misguided and their error is one of disobedience. They may be going down the highway in the wrong direction and thinking the problem is everyone else's.

Sometimes people in our society are stuck in an "emotional adolescence." Actually, some psychologists grimly posit that many, if not most, people do not grow emotionally beyond adolescence. Adolescents can be strident with black-and-white views and highly critical of any authority, beginning with their parents. Some priests are stuck in an emotional adolescence. They see the world in black-and-white terms, criticize their ecclesiastical superiors in strident and exaggerated ways, and see themselves as perpetual victims of the system. For these few priests, their rejection of authority and obedience stems from their own emotional deficits.

The other extreme is equally unhealthy, that is, the priest who becomes a passive sycophant. In this case, the priest stops thinking for himself and stops struggling with the truths of his faith. Instead of wrestling again and again, searching for a deeper, personal interiorization of the faith handed down by Jesus through his Church, he blindly parrots and agrees with whatever his superiors tell him. Whatever his motives, and for such priests there are many possible, he has done a disservice to himself and his Church. The Church needs mature, adult priests who can interact with their superiors as adults.

Of great importance for the mature priest is the old Latin phrase: *sentire cum ecclesia*, to think with the Church. The priest's heart and soul ought to be so formed in the years of his priesthood that his heart instinctively moves with the heart of the Church. This does not mean agreement on every institutional decision made by an organization staffed by humans, but it does mean that the priest has so attuned his spirit that he is in harmony with the one Spirit that moves the Church. Such a priest can never stray far or long from the truth.

A Healthy Obedience to the People of God

The priest's promise of obedience ought not stop with his obedience to Church authority and its teaching. The priest should be obedient, in some way, to the people whom he serves. It is a hallmark of some of the great saints that they exercised a kind of obedience to their peers and subordinates. This does not mean that we agree with or accept everything that is said to us or requested of us. This is a different kind of obedience. Rather, the priest as servant of the people is one whose life is subordinated to their authentic needs and spiritual welfare. His life is to be poured out in their service. This kind of obedience to others is a wonderful antidote to the narcissism and self-focus of our society. Some priests are infected with this societal affliction to a great degree; most of us have a bit of it. Obedience and service are the cure.

I have often thought that one of the first sentences out of a priest's mouth when a person walks into his office should be, "How may I help you?" The message is clear: He is there to serve. This attitude of service will help to dissipate any destructive clericalism and makes him accountable to the people whom he serves. Sadly, a few priests leave parishes in worse shape than when they arrived, fomenting discord and conflict during their tenure. While the priest cannot keep everyone happy, nor should he consider his role to be such, he is ordained to serve the people and to build a Christian community.

If a number of parishioners all give a priest the same feedback, he ought to pay particular attention to it. When the body of the faithful of his community rise up and give him some feedback or have a particular need or viewpoint, the priest ought to consider seriously whether this might be the Holy Spirit speaking to him. The married person has a spouse and children to provide feedback and perspective. For the priest, it is the community that he serves that ought to provide much of this feedback.

Thus, we priests need more ways to be held accountable and to receive direct feedback about our life and work. Such feedback helps us to live healthier lives. There are, in some dioceses, the beginnings of these accountability structures. In some dioceses, a pastor will receive written feedback at the end of his first term as pastor, usually about six years, from a sampling of selected parishioners.

Priests initially balk at the implementation of such evaluations, but, in the end, most find them very affirming. The vast majority of priests find out how much they are loved and appreciated. Sometimes they are given helpful ways to improve their lives and ministries. We all need to hear such suggestions. In a few cases, serious weaknesses surface and, if accepted in a spirit of obedient humility, it can be the occasion for considerable personal and spiritual growth.

These evaluations of pastors are only the beginning of the need for greater accountability structures, but they are a good start and I recommend such a process for every diocese. In dioceses or religious orders that do not have such a structure, a priest might consider initiating one for himself. At the end of a period of time, he could solicit written and verbal feedback from responsible members of the community that he serves. He might elect to sit down and review this data with the bishop, diocesan director of priest personnel, or another senior priest who can help him glean what he needs to take in from the information he is given. He may also want to sit down with the president of the parish council as well.

In our society, the virtue of obedience to authority is largely rejected. Even the place and validity of authority is questioned, if not completely rejected. The Christian faith, however, posits its importance. Our ultimate authority is, of course, God. This divine authority has been given to Jesus who, in turn, has entrusted it to his Church. We priests are thus given an important responsibility.

We ought to be reminded often that the authority that we possess is meant to be used in service. Because we are frail human beings, we need regular feedback from those whom we serve. In listening to them and responding to their needs, we exercise an obedience and selflessness that are essential. Similarly, we ought to exercise an obedient humility to our ecclesiastical superiors, as promised in our ordination, and to the teachings of the Church. Many would-be prophets have only been misguided individuals, stuck in their own erring views.

We have been blessed with a divinely revealed body of teaching and a focusing ministry of the successors of

Peter and the apostles. Exercising obedience to such divinely instituted authority not only is also a saving antidote to our own pride and narcissism, it is a wonderful grace. One of the great blessings of Catholicism is the Petrine ministry and its strong body of teaching. For we human beings who easily err, it is a sure compass that sets our sights directly toward the kingdom of God.

chapter 6

The Priestly Call to Passionate Living and Loving

To me, therefore, you shall be sacred; for I, the Lord, am sacred, I, who have set you apart from the other nations to be my own.

✠ Leviticus 20:26

I THINK IT WOULD BE A MISTAKE TO EITHER EXCORIATE celibacy or to launch into a soaring panegyric that describes more a life in heaven than the struggle of a life on earth. Celibate living does not warrant either. There are many other religions that extol the virtue of celibacy as a temporary or permanent state. These traditions include celibacy as part of a total religious self-giving and as a way of life conducive to living a focused spiritual life.

For example, Buddhism has a twenty-five-hundred-year history of a celibate spirituality. Likewise in Hinduism, *brahmacharya* or celibacy has long been an important part of its tradition, particularly for those devoted to God alone. There are ascetic philosophers who advocated celibate living, including Pythagoras who established a community of vegetarian celibates. Similarly, the Stoic philosopher Epictetus believed that the ideal teacher would be free from the entanglements of married life. "Celibacy has existed throughout religious history and in virtually all the major religions of the world."[24]

It is interesting that celibacy today attracts so much public attention and draws out so much emotion, especially from those who are not called to embrace it.

The call to celibacy is better served when the excessive emotion attracted to its mystique is deflated and it is looked at with a more sober eye.

In recent years, some have viewed mandatory celibacy as a sore spot in priestly morale. In my study, the priests were given the statement, "I support the requirement that priests live a celibate life." Slightly more than half, 53.2 percent, endorsed the statement. However, only 17.4 percent indicated that they would marry if given the chance. And 67.1 percent said, "Celibacy has been a positive experience for me." Thus, even with the much publicly maligned commitment to celibacy, a clear majority remain appreciative and contented. However, we ought to keep in mind that 33 percent of our brothers have not found it a positive experience. We ought to be sensitive to their struggle, willing to listen to their pain, and particularly solicitous for their welfare.

To live one's celibacy well, one must eventually see it in a positive light and appreciate the gifts that it brings. Sixty-seven percent of priests have done just that. To make the significance and strength of this finding more apparent, imagine giving the following statement to married couples throughout the United States: "Marriage has been a positive experience for me." Would 67 percent say yes?

Celibacy Not a Cause of Deviancy

But celibacy is excoriated in our culture and blamed for many of the ills within the Church. For example, many have suggested that the child sexual abuse crisis in the Church is connected to celibacy. Some have called for optional celibacy, citing the fact of child sex abuse by some clergy as a justification. However, no self-respecting researcher in the field of child sex abuse would suggest that celibacy is a cause for child sexual abuse. In fact, most child molesters in our society are, or will be, married. And for the few celibate priests who do molest minors, their psychological problems were long in place before they promised to live a celibate life. Such clinical problems are etched into the psyche at an early age.

Some have suggested that celibacy causes "sex starved" priests to engage in deviant sexual behavior. This, too, is transparently erroneous logic. Even if the priest was "sex starved," it would entice him to seek out an age-appropriate adult, not a child. The deviant sexual behavior that gives rise to the sexual abuse of children is a long-standing problem in an individual that predates seminary formation. In addition, while there are a few cases in which individuals have admitted choosing celibacy hoping it would cure their sexual problems, there are no indications that the incidence of child sexual abuse is any higher in the priesthood than in other male professions.[25] Simply put, celibacy neither causes child sexual abuse nor exacerbates its underlying deviant sexual tendencies.

The study *Sex in America* came up with an interesting finding. It was a study of the sexual behaviors of 3,432 Americans. In one part of the study, the researchers predicted that those who had the least genital sex would masturbate the most. Surprisingly, the study found just the opposite. Contrary to expectation, those who had the most sex masturbated the most. They wrote, "Our conclusion from these data is that masturbation is not a substitute for those who are sexually deprived, but rather it is an activity that stimulates and is stimulated by other sexual behavior."[26]

Absence of genital sex does not create sex-starved people. Rather, it is our sex-obsessed culture that spawns many who are compulsively sexual. As Patrick Carnes noted in his landmark work on sexual addictions, *Out of the Shadows*, one of the underlying or "core" beliefs of the sex addict, a belief that helps to give rise to the addiction, is: "Sex is my most important need."[27] This deviant core belief is reinforced constantly in our society and it gives birth to many sexual addictions.

One can only speculate why our sex-obsessed culture has developed such a negative obsession with celibacy. Certainly, the celibate represents a witness contrary to the one perpetrated by our society. The mere existence of a healthy and happy celibate must be a goad to a sex-obsessed world. There are millions of people in our society today who are caught up in sexually destructive, and often compulsive behaviors, such as internet cybersex, compulsive promiscuity, pornography, prostitution, and other sexual perversions. We should not be surprised. Individual pathology is spawned and grows in the cultural seedbed from which it springs. Since our society is obsessed with sex, and displays it incessantly and often in distorted ways, this sex-obsessed seedbed will naturally give rise to a plethora of people caught up in sexual problems.

The celibate Christian offers an important witness for today's world: There are some things more important than genital sex. People can, and many do, live in our world without a genital partner. What we cannot and should not live without is love, friendship, forgiveness, kindness, compassion, and many other true human needs. These essential needs are constitutive of humanity and thus, of course, of Christianity. These are the substance of the Christian life and must be cultivated by the celibate priest and by all Christians, married or otherwise.

At the same time, we do our priests a disservice when we speak of the celibate life in glowing, unrealistic terms. This is also true of our descriptions of marriage. No married couple who has been together for more than a couple of years wants to listen to someone extolling the bliss of marriage and idealizing the relationship. While marriage has many joys and wonderful blessings, it is also a challenge and a struggle, just as celibate living is a challenge and a struggle. Once again, it would be a mistake to look at the institution of marriage and suggest that it would solve the difficulties that face priesthood today. It would only be exchanging one set of problems for another.

There are, indeed, unique challenges in each vocation. For example, while all people struggle with loneliness, even married people, it is a particular struggle for the celibate priest. He is prone to succumbing to isolation and a resulting self-pity if he does not live his celibate commitment well. When vacation time comes and weekly days off approach, if the celibate is not careful he can find himself with nothing to do and very much alone. It is sad when a priest approaches his yearly vacation and discovers he has no friends with whom to share a few days of recreation.

In my survey, I decided to ask priests about their experience of loneliness. Only 6.6 percent of priests acknowledged feeling lonely "all" or "most" of the time. On the contrary, 80.7 percent said they have close friendships with other priests. While loneliness can be a particular trial for priests, the large majority report coping well.

Celibacy: A Yes to Passionate Relating

The celibate commitment is not simply a no to marriage, children, and genital relationships. So many get hung up with the no of celibacy and they miss its important yes. Stuck in the word no, the celibate eventually becomes bitter and resentful. He is angry because his personal life is based upon what is taken away from him. He is resentful, either consciously or unconsciously, because he feels he has been unjustly deprived of what is rightfully his. Indeed, he *has been* unjustly deprived if all celibacy means to him is no.

What then is the yes of celibacy? First of all, it should be affirmed that celibacy lived with integrity does not admit of a "third way." The celibate cannot be engaged in a sexual physical relationship with another person, even if that person is not married. Romantic kissing, fondling, and other such behaviors are incompatible with a celibate life and ought to be reserved for a romantic relationship. Occasionally I meet priests and religious who have distorted celibacy and interpret it as follows: "It only means I can't get married," or they rationalize their sexual activity with such phrases as: "These physical relationships are actually just a warm intimacy which everyone needs, including priests; it is not a violation of celibacy."

I spoke to a couple of priests who were living "double lives," that is, having a hidden sexually active life and still publicly functioning as priests. One of them spoke of it as "grinding away" his inner life. It was tearing him apart inside and slowly eroding his self-esteem. The other said similar things; the inner conflict was tearing him apart. He was on the verge of leaving the priesthood because a lack of integrity was slowly destroying his sense of vocation. Fortunately, both had been referred for help and were struggling, with assistance, to change their lives.

Authentic celibate living does not allow for double lives; it also does not allow for coupled relationships. One bishop complained that he had more than one priest in his diocese whom he described as living in "dry marriages." What he meant was that the priests were in an exclusive relationship with adult women that had all the trappings of a marriage, except there were no indications that the relationships were being acted out genitally. They were constantly together during the day and in the evenings. They ate most of their meals together and vacationed together. They were living coupled lives. Simply abstaining from genital sex does not mean one is living a life of integrity as a celibate.

The statement I like to use is this: Apply the *grandmother rule*. What would your or someone else's grandmother say if she saw you engaged in such behavior? I suspect our grandmothers might have something to say to these priests.

Moreover, the sex abuse crisis of 2002 has many things to teach us. One of these, first and foremost, is that the People of God, and for that matter all the people, expect Roman Catholic priests to live a life of integrity. They expect us to be the celibate, chaste, humble servants that we profess to be. Among other things, the crisis is a call to return to a life of integrity. The sexual laxity of the 1970s and '80s is over.

But celibacy cannot be lived in a kind of "white knuckle" fashion, hanging on for dear life, hoping not to violate one's chastity. There are more than a few who do this. Some stay away from others, fearful that a loving relationship could not be controlled. Others hide behind their work, their position, or a search for power, never really becoming involved with others until they reach mid-life when they feel an overpowering emptiness. The latter are prone to dysfunctional behaviors of a myriad of kinds, including sexual compulsiveness.

Celibate living is a yes, a yes that is to be lived out with passion and enthusiasm. Celibacy is not life-denying. In fact, the celibate priest is called to embrace all that is good in our world and all that gives witness to the goodness of God. There is much around us that gives witness to God.

It might seem safer for the celibate to live a kind of passionless life. I recall a chancery official who suggested it was better for celibates not to pay any attention to their sexuality. He thought it was better, and safer, to put sexuality behind you and move on. However, my experience suggests that such people might be "safer" for a while, but eventually trouble happens.

I remember a television commercial that showed a garage mechanic covered by grease with a huge wrench in his hand. Holding up the wrench, he looked directly at the audience and said, "You can pay me now, or you can pay me later." The implication was: If you wanted to fix it later, it would cost *a lot more*. You are better off paying attention to it now before it becomes a major issue. It is the same with our passion and sexuality. If we try to stuff it, hoping it will go away, the results are likely to be disastrous. I know of more than a few such cases.

Even if one is able to "white knuckle" it through life, I think it likely that the look on one's face will slowly turn to a bitter scowl. The celibate priest who denies his passion and sexuality, and lives an isolated, deadened life will naturally become bitter and angry. The heart has its own seasons and its own reasons. If it is denied genital sex, it can do just fine. If it is denied human warmth, kindness, and a passionate, committed life, it will shrivel up in anger and bitterness.

The sexuality and passion normally expressed in married sexual relations must be, for the celibate, channeled into a passionate life of pastoral love and relating. The questions that ought to be posed to each priest are: "How are you being nurtured and cared for?" and "Where is your passion?" A priest who lives a nurturing and nurtured life, and is passionate about his life, his faith, and his priesthood is likely to be a healthy person. His face cannot scowl for long, but ends up with a radiant smile. And there is no better vocational promotion than a happy priest.

Why Priests Leave

In the 2000 NFPC study of newly ordained priests, the first conclusion drawn was that the vast majority of newly ordained are happy in the priesthood and doing fine. In fact, in the companion study of priestly attitudes also sponsored by NFPC, there has been a steady rise in morale since the studies began in 1970. These have been primarily due to "a large rise in happiness among younger priests," the 25- to 45-year-olds.[28]

But when they surveyed and then interviewed those young priests who did resign, a common theme emerged. It wasn't their ministerial lives. They found ministry to be very satisfying. It wasn't even celibacy per se. Rather, resigned priests felt lonely, isolated, unappreciated, and/or disconnected. These personal difficulties made them very vulnerable to seeking out a coupled relationship.[29]

This conclusion only makes sense. It is likely that a few of the newly ordained that left should never have been ordained in the first place. However, a healthy celibate life must include strong interpersonal connections. The isolated priest is headed for a fall. Even if he does not leave the priesthood, both his psychological and his spiritual health will be seriously compromised. The sacred scriptures challenge us, "for whoever does not love a brother whom he has seen cannot love God whom he has not seen" (1 Jn 4:20).

Moreover, the priest who cannot form solid relationships would be mistaken if he believes that marriage will solve his problems. Our married people know full well how difficult and challenging a marital relationship is. Even the healthiest of people must labor hard to make a marriage work.

Celibate Relationship to God

What then are these celibate relationships that are so vital to the life of a priest? Mentioned first and foremost should be a relationship to God. Chapter Four, "The Priest as a Friend of God," spoke directly about the centrality of our friendship with God. It is integral to the identity of all Christians, but especially to the priest dedicated to God. *Celibacy and priesthood are both predominately spiritual realities.* It is true that psychology and the human sciences can help us understand and live certain aspects of priesthood and celibacy. But, in the end, one cannot fully understand or do justice to either without referring to the sacred sciences. Both priesthood and celibacy are rooted in the spiritual life and in a relationship to God. Thus, without a budding relationship with God, neither are understood or accepted. Perhaps this is an important reason why both priesthood and celibacy are so little understood and underappreciated in today's society.

One of the greatest impetuses to living a celibate life is being touched by, and then responding directly to, the love of God. This may sound like something from the great mystics, but recall that over 64 percent of newly ordained confirm that they had "an experience of spiritual awakening in [their] youth or adult years" that was "important for [their] vocation."[30] After being touched by the fire of God's love, the desire to live a celibate life, a life focused on God, is very understandable. It is not that all celibates have such a direct, powerful experience, but many do. Given the secularism of today's wealthy societies, the words of Karl Rahner transmit an important truth: "It has already been pointed out that the Christian of the future will be a mystic or he will not exist at all."[31]

For those who seek God earnestly and with persistence, I am convinced that God will, in some way, offer to them a direct experience of divine love. I worked for several months with a priest who suffered from scrupulosity. He had an imbedded belief that he was bad and that God was angry with him and judged him negatively. Such scrupulosity arose from his family environment; his father was angry and judgmental. He grew up believing he was never good enough. While we made some progress in therapy, he could not shake the idea that God was displeased with him, despite his living an exemplary life. So, I asked him to pray daily for a direct experience of God's love. Day after day, he prayed for such a grace. Finally, in a series of graced moments, he experienced how much God loves him and how pleased God is with him. This was an important healing experience.

With or without such powerful experiences, a steady living of a spiritual life and thus fostering one's relationship to God is essential. It is not accidental that the Twelve Steps of Alcoholics Anonymous have a strong spiritual focus. In many ways, their program of recovery is essentially a spiritual one. When working with priests who have strayed for a long period of time, it is rare to find their spiritual lives intact.

Deism easily infects our Christian faith. As noted previously, the deist believes that God created the universe and now watches it from a distance, letting it run on its own. This is not Christianity. While it is true that God has given natural laws to govern our universe, a basic tenet of Christianity is that God has become incarnate in our world in the person of Jesus. Thus, God has entered our existence and is, even now, filling us with the divine life. "And behold, I am with you always, until the end of the age" (Mt 28:20).

Thus, the celibate life is a witness to this Christian reality, that is, God is with us. Jesus told us plainly, "At the resurrection they neither marry nor are given in marriage but are like angels in heaven" (Mt 22:30). However, the next life is already here in its beginning form, because God is now with us and in us, that is, the "kingdom of God is at hand." The celibate life is a living witness of this kingdom already begun. It defies our common sense because it is not natural. Indeed, it is not natural; it is *super*-natural. In Jesus, the *super*-natural has already begun, here and now.

For this witness to be healthy and effective, the celibate must have a relationship with God who is present now. Deism is not a life-giving option. In the survey I conducted, it was edifying to note that 94 percent professed to "have a personal relationship with God (or Jesus) that is nourishing to me." The response was almost unanimous. Priests do not speak much about their personal relationship with God. We tend to be very private about our personal spiritual journeys, perhaps a bit too much so. But the survey results show that our priests' relationships to God are thriving and are an important part of their lives.

Celibate Relationship to Others

Like his relationship to God, the celibate priest's relationship to others is also important. An isolated priest is one headed for a fall, as the 2000 NFPC study showed. But we priests have to work at our relationships. They do not just happen. If we are not careful, we will spend all of our time ministering to others and neglecting ourselves.

While such a life might seem selfless, it is ultimately self-destructive. When our day off comes, we will find ourselves alone. When troubles strike, we have no one to share our burdens. Priesthood easily becomes a lonely life if we passively let it happen.

Thus, we must work at our relationships. We must actively cultivate a network of real friends. Too many of us think that our acquaintances are friends. Most priests have a lot of acquaintances. They know a little bit about us and we know a little bit about them. We see them from time to time and we might occasionally enjoy their company. But friendship is more than that. Friends share their joys and their burdens. They speak of their sorrows and their hopes. Friends are vulnerable with each other. And there is a nurturing and mutually supporting quality to their relationship.

Here is a simple litmus test of whether or not you have any friends. Think of the most difficult struggle you are going through at this time . . . it could be something physical, spiritual, or psychological. Regardless of what your biggest struggle is now, the question I pose is: Whom have you told? Have you shared this with anyone? Friends share their struggles and receive support.

I know that we men are not very good at sharing personal things. It is not essential for friendship that we share everything. But the man—or woman—who is a closed book and shares little if anything might question whether he or she has any true friends.

Fortunately, the ability to make friends is not a genetic quality. It is a learned skill. Anyone can make friends and it is never too late. I remember doing a psychological assessment of a priest and asking him if he had any friends. He responded, "No, no one ever calls me." I responded, "Does the phone in your rectory only work one way? You could call someone else." His response to this question was revealing, "What if I call someone and that person says no?" Here was the nub of it: The priest was afraid of rejection. Friendship involves risk. We open ourselves to another and make ourselves vulnerable. Indeed, the other person can say no. And if that happens, it will hurt a bit. But the wound is not fatal and we can try again with another.

After being questioned about friendships, another priest said, "There is no one interested in being my friend." Underneath the bravado and seeming confidence of some in their priestly roles are a tenuous self-esteem and pervasive fear. These men are good at helping others and functioning in their roles, but when placed with peers, they feel inadequate and unwanted.

The good news is that there are people who want to become our friends if only we give them a chance. When we feel unlovable and unwanted, it is our own inner demons that are speaking. If we but reach out to others, all of us will find connection and, eventually, friendship. We are swimming in a sea of human needs, emotions, and potential intimacies. For those who see only emptiness and isolation around them, I encourage them to believe that their perspective and their lives can change.

After working a number of years with priests and religious who have a multitude of psychological problems, the road to recovery almost always involves a reconnection with others. Rebuilding human relationships is almost always a constitutive part of healing and changing one's life. Healing is not accomplished in isolation.

Seminary formation of future priests does not typically include explicit instruction and fostering of human friendships. No vocation that I am aware of does include such instruction. Given my experience of working with priests who have had difficulties, I recommend that it be included. While all walks of life thrive best in a climate of nurturing relationships, healthy celibacy demands a life of passionate relating.

Boundaries

When discussing the issue of priestly relationships, the issue of boundaries naturally surfaces. When people use the word boundaries they usually mean what things we should *not* do. It is discussed only in its negative sense, that is, the nos. But boundaries are about both yes and no. As the scriptures tell us, "Let your 'Yes' mean 'Yes,' and your 'No' mean 'No'" (Mt 5:37). With proper boundaries, we say yes to those with whom we want to be in closer relationship, and no to those people and situations we ought to keep at a healthy distance.

The priest who only knows how to say yes will eventually end up in situations and relationships where he ought not to be. On the other hand, for the priest who only can say no, his life will be a safe but sterile bubble.

Good boundaries are difficult, especially in the midst of a very intense and emotionally complex life, such as that of an active priest. He is surrounded by many people with many needs. At times, his own needs can confound an already overwhelming picture. For example, with the death of a priest's parents and the onset of mid-life, a priest understandably can become more vulnerable to inappropriate relationships. He may end up looking for comfort in improper places. Once again, the *grandmother rule* might be helpful. If your grandmother saw what you were doing, what would she say?

Boundaries are also important in keeping negative influences out and carving out space for a personal life.

Every priest eventually has a small number of people who approach him in inappropriate ways. For example, some people will want him to spend an inordinate amount of time with them. Others will call him or ask to see him at all hours for inconsequential things. A few will even test his boundaries to see if he is willing to engage in a sexual relationship. Without healthy boundaries, his life will quickly spin out of control.

Similarly, the priest himself needs a personal life. The one who is constantly and forever on duty denies himself necessary personal time for rest, recreation, study, and spiritual regeneration. It reminds me of the priest whose personal life was falling apart. When asked, "Do you take a day off each week?" he responded with an underlying tone of anger, "No, I can't. There is always someone needing my attention." Ironically, his erroneous belief that he was indispensable resulted in his inability to provide for the people, at least for several months until he got back on his feet.

There needs to be a way for the priest to place a boundary between his ministry and a personal life. Some are able to do this within the context of a rectory attached to the church. Usually, the priest's personal quarters are "off limits" to all but his friends. With the decreasing numbers of priests and increasing number of paid and volunteer staff, some rectories have been converted into offices and the priest(s) lives a short distance away in a house owned by the parish. This is a particularly effective way to separate ministry and personal space.

Saying "No" Well

One skill every priest needs to learn, and one that ought to be taught in the seminary, is the art of saying "no" well. The longer a priest stays in an assignment and the more popular he is among people, the more nos he will have to say. Most priests find it personally difficult to say no. As a result, the tendency is to become swamped with work. For a few others, their lives and negative demeanors say no without ever opening their mouths. These are angry and bitter men. Their boundaries are too rigid.

I learned to say no from my sister-in-law. I overheard a phone conversation she had once. Someone was asking her to chair a benefit. She is a good organizer, connects well with people, and is often in demand. Thus, she cannot satisfy all the requests that come her way. When the phone conversation ended, she had said no in such a way that she affirmed the other person, kept their relationship alive and well, but gently communicated that she was not able to do it.

Summarizing her approach, I have put together several basic steps to use when saying no:

Step 1: Affirm the project.

Step 2: Express your honor at being asked to participate.

Step 3: Say you would love to be involved if you could.

Step 4: Communicate that you are sorry, but that you are not able to do so. It is not necessary to give reasons why.

For example, if someone asks you to take the high school group to the museum, you might say, "It is a wonderful thing to take our young people to the museum. I know that they will learn a lot and enjoy themselves as well. I am honored that you would think of me and ask me. I would love to be involved if I could. But, I am sorry that I am not able to do so. But I certainly wish you well and I hope it is a great trip."

To live a celibate life well as a priest is not for the faint-hearted. It requires someone courageous enough to say yes to a passionate life of living and loving. It also requires us to say no much more often than we would like. Our priests need training in learning both how to say yes and to build relationships, and knowing when and how to say no.

The Gift That Is Celibacy

With the declining support for celibacy in our sex-obsessed society, the need for its witness is all the greater. But living it is also more difficult. No longer are we priests surrounded by people who support, or even appreciate, its value. If we are to live it well, the times demand that we take it into our hearts and find there an energy and an enthusiasm for this grace-filled, but difficult, calling. The stakes are high; if we find such an enthusiasm we are likely to become joy-filled and passionate priests. If not, we are prone to becoming angry and bitter men.

The gift comes in many kinds of packages, each unique to the addressee. Some priests speak of the gift of his being present and available to the people. These great shepherds of souls find joy and nourishment in their relationships with the people they serve. Other priests speak of the gift in their direct and unfettered relationship to God. They are the contemplatives among us whom we badly need. Still other priests experience directly the power of the sacraments and focus their celibate priesthood on these graced moments. These priests are conduits of Christ's saving grace. Upon closer reflection, there are some of all three charisms in each of us.

Sometimes we should take the words of the scriptures as literally true:

> Peter began to say to him, "We have given up everything and followed you." Jesus said, "Amen, I say to you, there is no one who has given up house or brothers or sisters or mother or father or children or lands for my sake and for the sake of the gospel who will not receive a hundred times more now in this present age . . . and eternal life in the age to come" (Mk 10:28–30).

Priesthood is not a part-time commitment. It cannot be lived half-heartedly. It is an all-consuming vocation because the call we have heard to follow Jesus is an all-consuming one. It admits of no distraction or competition. Celibacy is but one moment in this personal and total self-commitment.

Jesus promised us eternal life in the age to come. But he also promised us one hundredfold in this life. We have already received this bounty and continue to receive it. We have received one hundred times as many brothers and sisters, families, and homes than we could ever have imagined. Jesus has been true to his word and we have been richly blessed.

chapter 7

The Priest as a Male: In an Era of the Ascending Feminine

It was told of Abbot John the Dwarf that once he had said to his elder brother: "I want to live in the same security as the angels have, doing no work, but serving God without intermission." And casting off everything he had on, he started out into the desert. When a week had gone by he returned to his brother. And while he was knocking on the door, his brother called out before opening, and asked: "Who are you?" He replied: "I am John." Then his brother answered and said, "John has become an angel and is no longer among men. . . . If you are a man, you are going to have to start working again in order to live. . . ." So John did penance and said: "Forgive me, brother, for I have sinned."[32]

✣ Thomas Merton

THE PRIEST IS FIRST A MAN. POPE JOHN PAUL II, IN HIS landmark work on priestly formation, *Pastores Dabo Vobis,* speaks clearly and forcefully about the importance of human formation. This apostolic exhortation reads, "The whole work of priestly formation would be deprived of its necessary foundation if it lacked a suitable human formation."[33] To be an effective priest, he must first be a balanced human being.

Since he is a man, he therefore must have the balanced psyche of a man. But this is not as obvious and simple as it first might appear, especially in the Western culture of today. I believe there is an underlying subtle, and sometimes not-so-subtle, negativism toward maleness today. I saw a bumper sticker that read, "To succeed, a woman has to work twice as hard as a man. Fortunately, that isn't difficult." Old television sitcoms that exalted the place of the male such as "Father Knows Best" have been replaced with the likes of "Men Behaving Badly."

Where did this negativism toward men come from? It is very likely that it is a backlash from centuries of male dominance and discrimination toward women. As quoted earlier, the famous church historian, Msgr. John Tracy Ellis, said in one of his lectures that today's anti-clericalism is a direct result of the clericalism of the past. Similarly, I suspect that today's anti-masculinity is a strong reaction to the male dominance of the past. Today's men are suffering for the sins of their fathers. If one were to capture the former spirit of male dominance in a phrase, one might use a line from the musical *My Fair Lady*: "Why can't a woman be more like a man?" It has been replaced with a new mantra: "Why can't a man be more like a woman?"

Within this cultural bias against masculinity and maleness, the priest as a man needs to be courageous enough to welcome his masculinity, embrace it, and express it in a balanced way. This might be difficult in this climate, but it is nonetheless one of his tasks. Ironically, the priest who is not able to embrace his masculinity in a positive way is prone to lapsing into one of two destructive extremes. He may either repress his masculinity and become "wishy-washy" and indecisive, feeling guilty and apologizing for his maleness, or he may fall into the other extreme, becoming aggressive, power-hungry, and domineering.

Becoming a mature male means being comfortable with one's masculinity and thus not needing either to hide it or to exaggerate it. We ought not apologize for being a man. At the same time, we should not use our masculinity as a weapon.

Masculinity Versus Femininity

When speaking of masculinity, I am not referring to gender identity per se, that is, whether one is biologically a man or a woman. Rather, masculinity encompasses a set of personality traits and ways of interacting with others and with the world that are associated with men today. These traits are found in varying degrees in both women and men. The same would apply to femininity traits and women. Not surprisingly, masculinity traits are typically found in greater degree in men and feminine traits are often stronger in women, but men and women have some of both.

When defining the traits associated with masculinity and femininity today, one might use varying lists. To define masculinity, I will be referring to such traits as rational, leadership, intellectual, competitive, assertive, task-oriented, identity in uniqueness, and obedient to hierarchy. Stereotypical feminine traits might be relational, nurturing, warm, inclusive, gentle, emotional, caring, and collaborative. As we can see, each of us has all of these to a varying degree, but the masculine traits tend to be associated with the stereotypical man and the feminine traits are associated with the stereotypical female.

It should be obvious that all of these masculine and feminine traits listed, when exercised in moderation, are good qualities to have. So, one set of traits is not better than the other. But they do emphasize different ways of relating to others and to the world. A danger would be to label some of these traits as good and others as bad, or more or less desirable. Unfortunately, this is the case.

Each set of traits has its own downside. When not balanced by other-gender traits and thus taken only by themselves, they can become a caricature and result in gender "poisoning." The macho man who has no relational skills or warmth is as dysfunctional as the passive, overly emotional woman who is unable to assert herself. They are stereotypes badly in need of some other-gender traits.

The dark side of masculinity has a number of typical symptoms. For example, unbalanced masculinity can result in restricted emotionality. Many males are unable to express their emotional selves, except perhaps with the one "acceptable" male emotion: anger. Softer feelings of tenderness, grieving, and warmth are repressed. This is typical of many households: Dad can get angry, but he is not supposed to cry.

Other symptoms of masculinity gone awry include the need to be in control. Psychic defenses of rationalization and intellectualization are used to an extreme. Also, a healthy competitiveness is replaced by grasping for power and the desire to dominate.

In relationships, excessive masculinity is often expressed in a fear of dependence and in an isolated independence, that is, "I can do it myself." The excessive male often interprets intimacy only to mean genital sex. Thus, celibacy is particularly difficult for the masculine-extreme male. Instead of being able to form nurturing, nongenital relationships, he is stuck with one of two extremes, being genitally active or being in a cold isolation.

I recall working with more than one priest who had difficulty in living a chaste life. I asked each of them about friendships and relationships in their lives. Some responded that they were not able to engage in relationships because they are called to be celibate. I told them, "There is something in between genital relationships and isolation." The typical response was, "What?" For many of these men, they do not have an inkling or any personal experience of warm, nongenital, chaste friendships. The good news is that such relationships can be learned . . . but only if one is willing to engage in "feminine" kinds of traits such as sharing, vulnerability, and connection. For some, this can be very threatening.

On the other hand, there is a dark side to femininity as well, that is, to unrestricted femininity not balanced with masculine traits. Some of these include becoming passive and neglecting self for others. The excessive feminine is not able to engage in healthy assertive behavior and may resort to being passive-aggressive. This person is also unable to care for self because her needs are repressed in favor of others. As a result, she might lose her own identity and cling to relationships with others in a codependent fashion.

I have worked with more than a few women religious who suffered from such difficulties. As they learn to value themselves and their own needs, and to express these needs in an assertive way, they find their self-esteem rising and gain a sense of self-efficacy. They learn to find their own voice.

God has so created the human race that males and females need each other, just as masculinity and femininity become warped without the other.

The Age of the Feminine

Chicago priest Father Lou Cameli in a 1993 speech at the National Conference of Diocesan Vocation Directors convention cited Patrick Arnold's work on masculine spirituality and his sense of the ascendancy of the dynamic feminine in our age. This has had a significant impact on the life of the church and its ministry. Father Cameli noted a shift from patterns of ministry that were stereotypically masculine to the currently dominant feminine models. Thus, our approach to ministry and spirituality has become excessively feminine with little balance from the masculine.

To test his hypothesis, I conducted an informal study of a group of 115 priests. I gave them 18 traits, half of which were typically considered as feminine and half of which were considered masculine.[34] I asked them to choose the traits from of this list that they considered most desirable. The first nine they chose were feminine traits; only the last one was a masculine trait. It was striking how the feminine traits were overwhelmingly considered much more desirable. It would have been interesting if the same test was conducted 50 years ago in the age of the dominant masculine. I suspect the results would have been very different.

Femininity and masculinity lead to very different ways of approaching ministry, spirituality, and theology. Being in the age of the dominant feminine, a feminine approach to all these is currently in vogue in many areas.

For example, in ministry a feminine approach emphasizes such good pastoral values as being person-centered, connecting with others, nurturing and caring, being inclusive, sharing responsibility, and using a team approach. Even listing these values, one can see how much they dominate modern ministry and how truly important they are. The priest who cannot support such values is liable to be ineffective and he will quickly become an anachronism. The age of the autocratic pastor is over.

But if such values are not balanced with masculine ministerial values, it can easily lead to difficulties. For example, there are times in a parish when appropriate authority and leadership must be exercised. The pastor will need to make difficult decisions from time to time and these decisions will not always be popular. Would the pastor want to leave the decision to a consensus of the parish council about whether the parish will support Church teachings on abortion and contraception? Of course not. Similarly, there are times the pastor will not only want to nurture parishioners, he will also want to challenge them. Thus, nonpracticing, engaged couples who present themselves to the pastor and wish to be married in a week because they have already rented the reception hall are not likely to be given a positive response, and rightly so. The pastor not only nurtures and includes, he also challenges and exercises leadership.

A masculine model of ministry might be described as being task-oriented, challenging, clear and predictable, productive and efficient, fostering identity in uniqueness, a healthy competitiveness, well-defined leadership, and loyalty to hierarchy. Such masculine values have been descending in importance in many areas.

A Declining Masculine Theology

One can readily see the damaging results to ministry and theology in this age of the decline of masculinity. In modern times, we have emphasized such good theological values as God's forgiveness and mercy as well as God's love and closeness to our humanity. Likewise, we have emphasized that human beings are good and made in God's image. These naturally flow from a feminine theological approach. These are all true and important theological values that need to be preached. They are an important antidote to the earlier masculine era in which sinfulness and the reality of God's judgment and hell were preached with gusto in parish missions and from the pulpit. Many older parishioners will relate how they feel scarred by such negative images of self and such harsh, judging images of God.

But, as a result of moving so far away from any masculine values and almost totally embracing the feminine, I believe that there has been a tendency to downplay important theological truths. These truths are necessary for a balanced preaching of the Gospel of Jesus.

Thus, as we have emphasized the love and mercy of God, the reality of sin and evil has almost been eclipsed. The sacrament of reconciliation is often underutilized, the reception of communion no longer appears to be tied to a state of grace, and many do not believe in the existence of a personified evil, that is, Satan. It is not surprising that many do not believe in the existence of hell. Or, if they do, they are apt to believe that few souls, if any, end up there.

In short, the masculine "teeth" have been removed from our religion. The portrayal of God these days reminds one of the actor George Burns who played "God" in a series of movies. He showed himself to be a nice, kindly old grandfather. Today, we often hear of the love of God, but we have lost the divine majesty, power, and awesome grandeur. We have lost an appropriate sense of reverential fear. "It is a fearful thing to fall into the hands of the living God" (Heb 10:31).

In this era of the declining masculine, the impetus to evangelize and convert has waned. Since we have so emphasized universal human goodness and tried to promote ecumenism and inclusion, which are all feminine values, it makes little sense to try to convert others to our religion. After all, why convert someone if there is no hell, no need for redemption, and no need to renounce evil and turn away from sin?

Pope John Paul II rightly called the Church back to the "masculine" values of evangelization in his 1990 encyclical *Redemptoris missio*. The Holy Father wrote of "an undeniable negative tendency" today that weakens the Church's mission to evangelize. He called us a missionary activity that "revitalizes. . . Christian identity," another masculine value: identity in uniqueness![35]

Given these trends, it is little wonder that the Congregation for the Doctrine of the Faith's declaration of 2000, entitled *Dominus Jesus*, received so much negative press. While it could be argued that the document needed to be more sensitively worded (i.e., be more couched in "femininity"), its masculine approach to the faith offered an important antidote to modern excesses.

In particular, *Dominus Jesus* spoke clearly and directly of several major truths that are not popular today. First, Jesus alone is Lord and Savior. Buddha may have been a holy man and Mohammed may have been a prophet, but there is one Lord and one Savior. "There is no salvation through anyone else, nor is there any other name under heaven given to the human race by which we are to be saved" (Acts 4:12). I often repeat this truth to groups of priests. I speak a very masculine, assertive, and challenging statement, "If you do not believe it, you are not a Christian." To the modern inclusive mentality, "not wishing to offend" approach, this seems horribly harsh. But, it is the truth. It is a truth we need to hear.

Second, *Dominus Jesus* repeated another important truth. While the "Catholic Church rejects nothing of what is true and holy in these (other) religions,"[36] the "fullness of Christ's salvific mystery belongs . . . to the Church." The Church, founded by Jesus, "subsists in the Catholic Church, governed by the Successor of Peter and by the Bishops in communion with him." The Church of Christ "continues to exist fully only in the Catholic Church."[37] The truths in these statements have long been integral to the Catholic faith. They are expressed in what I am calling masculine terms and seem exclusive and harsh to the modern feminine mentality. But I say to our priests, "If you do not believe this about the Catholic Church, you are not in harmony with its fundamental teachings."

One can easily see how such truths naturally give impetus to the mission of evangelization. If only Jesus saves, and the fullness of the revelation and presence of Christ subsists only in the Catholic Church, then we are on fire with a spirit of evangelization. Our task becomes urgent. We want to call and urge people to be saved. We want them to come to know the fullness of Jesus and his saving mystery. Indeed, this evangelical urgency is the perspective of the Gospels. "The light will be among you only a little while. Walk while you have the light, so that darkness may not overcome you" (Jn 12:35). And again we are urged, "Enter through the narrow gate; for the gate is wide and the road broad that leads to destruction. . . . How narrow the gate . . . that leads to life. And those who find it are few" (Mt 7:13–14). Our theology and pastoral practice have emphasized the feminine with a concomitant decline in the more masculine aspects of theology. It is little wonder that one can perceive in the Church today a budding movement toward reintegrating the masculine. There is an amorphous group of people who are calling for "old" values to be reintegrated in our Church. They speak of the reality of sin in the world and the work of Satan. They warn people of damnation and speak of God's coming judgment. They reverence the leadership of the bishops and priests. They urge people to convert and join the church.

While we would not want to return to the days of a masculine-only perspective which led some into a guilt-ridden scrupulosity, we would do well to listen to this resurgence of the masculine and reintegrate it, in a balanced way, into today's church.

Toward a Gender-Integrated Church

When society, and thus Church, becomes unbalanced in its approach to gender, it suffers from extremes. If previous generations leaned toward an excessive masculinity, the current one suffers from an unbalanced dominance of the feminine. We see it in the popular culture and in our society at large. We see it in the Church as well.

The truth is not "either or" but "both and." Our God has attributes of masculinity and femininity. God is all-powerful and a just judge. God is also loving, compassionate, and merciful. Human beings were indeed created good and are loved by God. But they are also mired in sin and can only be saved by the death and resurrection of one person, Jesus Christ.

We need all the sacraments. Not only do we need to emphasize such sacraments as Baptism and Eucharist, as we do today, but we also need to recover the importance of the "lost sacraments" of today: the sacraments of Reconciliation and the ordained priesthood. We recognize that we are all sinners and need forgiveness and healing; these come to us sacramentally and directly through the Church's ministry, that is, through the instrumentality of its ordained priests. It is our privilege to be ministers of these truths.

While we rightly recognize the goodness that is found in other religions, we do not hesitate to call others to convert to Christ and to become members of the Catholic Church. We want them to be saved. We want them to come to the fullness of the revelation of Jesus found in the Catholic Church. We need not apologize for our evangelical spirit.

We priests do not need to apologize for being men as well. It is a gift to be a man, just as it is a gift to be a woman. We rejoice in the masculinity that God has given us. We do not apologize for being assertive and competitive. We strive to be good leaders and to use our reason and intellect well. We are not afraid to speak of the presence of sin and evil in the world and the need for repentance. We, as mature adults, hold obedience to the Church as a virtue.

Just as we want our Church to integrate both the feminine and the masculine, so, too, must we do the same in our own lives and in ourselves. Each of us will have varying degrees of the masculine and the feminine in our lives, but all of us will strive to have a balance of both. We priests want to be strong and yet gentle; we strive to be assertive without being judgmental; we want to be evangelizers as well as ecumenical; we want to be independent and yet also men of communion.

Much of the bickering in the church today is from radicalized groups condemning others. Pope John Paul II himself spoke about these factions to the U.S. bishops at their 2004 *ad limina* visit:

> As in any family, the Church's internal harmony can at times be challenged by a lack of charity and the presence of conflict among her members. This can lead to the formation of factions within the Church. . . . Bishops are charged to act with fatherly solicitude as men of communion to ensure that their particular Churches act as families, so "that there may be no discord in the body."[38]

Each group has many good things to say, but they err in their narrowness. They are not fully Catholic because they are not in communion with the entire church, but only with the part of the church they choose to accept. We priests will want to eschew extremist positions that emphasize one aspect of the faith but downplay others. We will invite and challenge such individuals into full communion with the Catholic Church. We do not profess ourselves to be liberal or conservative, members of the left wing or the right, or members of any other limiting group. Rather, we call ourselves Catholic and proudly profess that the fullness of Christ subsists in our communion. It is in his name that we are saved.

chapter 8

The Priest as Man of Communion[39]

Of special importance is the capacity to relate to others. This is truly fundamental for a person who is called to be responsible for a community and to be a "man of communion."[40]

✠ JOHN PAUL II

WHAT HAS STRUCK ME FORCIBLY OVER THE PAST FEW years has been the intense, negative polarization of the Church today. Where there should be communion and dialogue, there is faction and diatribe. I remember one Sunday afternoon being on a news program with two people. The person on the left was promoting radical stances for the Church in a shrill demeanor and on the right was a man from the Catholic League. Those watching the show who were not Catholic must have shaken their heads and wondered how these two people could coexist in the same Church. In fact, if this Church of ours were not Catholic with all its attendant history, structure, theology, divine grace, and spirituality, it might be splintering into several denominations, as indeed some other churches do.

The very nature of our Catholic Church is that it is a place of communion. If it is truly a Catholic or universal Church, every element will not be the same and there will be a harmonious tension between them. Nevertheless, they are intertwined into a single body. What these past few years have suggested to me is not the presence of a communion, but rather that we are moving closer to factions. By factions I mean the absence of a respectful dialogue and the absence of a mutual acceptance. At times the exchanges between groups in our Church are more like diatribes with little real communication.

This was raised in high relief during the 2002 child sexual abuse crisis in the United States. At a time of crisis, a community is called to work together to face the problems. When a crisis strikes a family, the brothers and sisters, parents and children bond together even more strongly to face it with courage and combined strength. We have done just the opposite and embarked upon much name-calling and finger-pointing, including looking for scapegoats to blame.

One is rightly angered by anyone who sexually molests a child, especially by a priest and by those who support his heinous behavior. But, as a psychologist, I would say that the rage that has surfaced in this country, especially during (but not limited to) the aftermath of the crisis, seems deeper and broader. It is as if this crisis has tapped into a well of anger, distrust, and fear that has been simmering just below the surface. If there is a lack of dialogue and communion present now, each of us should look into our own hearts and ask ourselves how we have contributed to it.

Given the theological stature of such a great Catholic thinker as Cardinal Avery Dulles, his words on this subject bear repeating at some length:

> . . . the conflict between the liberal and conservative wings has markedly politicized the Church. Both sides are tempted to subordinate an even-handed concern for truth to the demands of a party spirit in which every action and statement is evaluated according to whether it supports one cause or the other. The Church as a universal communion is severely wounded by such partisanship. . . . The opposed parties seek to discredit their opponents, often by acrimonious attacks that are uncharitable and even unjust. . . . In spite of the agitation from both

> extremes, the Catholic Church remains a communion of tradition and authority, open to dialogue and progress. Thanks to its deposit of faith, it has the resources to cope with the modern crisis of truth.[41]

What is needed is a refinding of the communion and Christian community that is, of its very nature, what it means to be the Church. This points to a need for a deep, inner reconciliation in Christ. The American Heritage Dictionary defines "conciliate," the root of "reconciliation," as "to overcome the distrust or animosity of."[42] Factions and diatribes emerge from the heart inside each of us. These past few years have shown that when we look into our own hearts there is much anger, distrust, and animosity.

It might surprise and dismay us that in the psychological treatment of child sex abusers, one of the most common aspects of their pathology is an underlying anger, a kind of festering rage. It is hidden and eroticized, and often splits the psyche between the "good person" and the "bad person." The "bad person" remains hidden from consciousness and subtly rends the entire structure. Ironically, when we in the Church and in our wider society allow the rage in our own hearts to tear at the fiber of our community, to split us into factions that we designate good and bad, we are actually perpetuating the kind of dynamics that give rise to the sexual abuse of children. We then become part of the problem, not part of the solution. It is no accident that Jesus emphasized what lies in the heart, "You have heard that it was said to your ancestors, 'You shall not kill; and whoever kills will be liable to judgment.' But I say to you, whoever is angry with his brother will be liable to judgment" (Mt 5:21–22).

It is not that we should all think alike or that we should agree with everything that others say. No, there should be a healthy tension within our communion;

there ought to be an undulating exchange of ideas and perspectives that leads to a greater whole and a deepening unfolding of the boundless Truth who is God. But it should be a communion of dialogue. There should be a charity of brothers and sisters that marks our exchanges. The crisis has waned, but the underlying anger, distrust, and animosity have not. They surface again and again, in different venues, with different masks, and continue to spread their destructive poison.

What then are the qualities we ought to look for and foster in the priesthood? I would organize them around the words of John Paul II in *Pastores Dabo Vobis*. As noted in the opening of the chapter, he said that the priesthood is "radically communitarian," and that "of special importance is the capacity (of the priest) to relate to others. This is truly fundamental for a person who is called to be responsible for a community and to be a 'man of communion.'" This then is our answer. A priest is to be a "man of communion."

Today we priests face a divided Church and divided parishes. We have Hispanics and Vietnamese, Poles and Italians, Filipinos and Haitians. We have the "liturgical police" watching our every moment on the altar and conservatives screening our words for orthodoxy. We have liberals complaining about our pro-life homilies and our support of *Humanae Vitae*. We work side-by-side with homosexual people and heterosexual people, priests who wear cassocks and those who yearn for the "glory days of Vatican II." We have old people in nursing homes who nostalgically remember the Latin Mass and vehemently reject removing the communion rail, and young people who have never received communion on their tongues and think that the communion rail is a decoration. It will be easy for a priest, and very tempting, to align himself with one group or the other. Inevitably, some of this naturally occurs since our own predispositions will make us more sympathetic with some stances rather than others. But our vocation is to be a shepherd, a pastor of souls to all, regardless of their theological or cultural makeup, orientation, or age. The priest should be a "man of communion."

This will require that we have a heart big enough to welcome all. It does not mean that we need to agree with all. We owe it to the people to adhere faithfully to the teachings of the Church to which they belong and to which we belong. We must represent this Church with integrity. Also, we must have a special love for our bishop whom we look to with a mature obedience. The priest shares in the ministry of the bishop and sees in his bishop an important source of Catholicity and unity. The priest of today and tomorrow will want to transcend all factions to become truly Catholic, in the narrowest and broadest sense of that word. Our ministry is universal, just as Jesus called all people.

But this is incredibly difficult because it requires that in the very core of our hearts, there is a level of healing and holiness that only the very best of our pastors have achieved. Perhaps I have asked too much of a priest, but it must be a goal for which we strive. When our hearts are not able to include one group or another, when they subtly reject them, this rejected group under our care must inevitably feel disenfranchised. Such priests quickly splinter parishes. It may be that some of the current movement toward factions in our Church community stems from a feeling of being disenfranchised in our Church.

To make various factions feel welcomed, to be "[men] of communion," will require in us priests what I would call a *reconciled heart*. I propose four aspects to a reconciled heart, and once we consider these four elements, we will see how difficult a task it is. The first is this: *A reconciled heart has a solid sense of self-identity and a secure self-image*. When we are at peace with who we are, when we know and accept the person that God has made us, we are able to accept others with all their faults and weaknesses. A candidate who is stuck in a personal self-loathing would not be appropriate for ordination. Some have slipped through the formation process in the past. A lack of self-acceptance breeds an angry judgmentalism of others. I cannot but surmise that those priests who are so judgmental and negative toward others must, in some way, view themselves through the same negative judgmental filter.

When priests and sisters finish our healing program at Saint Luke Institute, I often ask them if they have experienced God in some way during their stay of several months. I have found it edifying and instructive to learn that many have had a direct and powerful experience of God. And the theme is almost always the same. They tell me that God came to them directly and personally and revealed to them just how much he loved them the way they were. These graces are received with joy-filled tears and are incredibly healing on every level.

Closely connected to the first aspect of a reconciled heart, a firm self-acceptance and solid self-identity, is the second aspect of a reconciled heart: *an integration of one's emotions and sexuality*.

The integration of one's sexuality is particularly difficult. But it demands that individuals know who they are sexually, live in peace with the sexual person that they are, and can express this sexuality in a way that is in consonance with their vocation. Thus, we priests need to express ourselves as sexual people in ways that are not genital or leading toward a genital relating, and yet fully alive and fully passionate. Celibates are not distant and cold, but passionate lovers who have developed the gift of celibate self-giving and receiving.

The issue of homosexuality in the seminaries and priesthood has surfaced amid much emotion and threatens to become an intense battleground. There are two fundamental positions that have been put forward. Each has something to add to the dialogue, I believe, but each is, by itself, inadequate. The first position is this: *The presence of any same sex-attractions in a candidate automatically precludes him from priestly ministry*. Such a statement is too broad and is not the tradition of our Church. Distinctions need to be made. Many persons with same-sex attractions are, indeed, not appropriate candidates for the seminary, such as those with significant histories of sexual behaviors, or those who dissent from the Church's teaching on human sexuality, or those whose inner sexual conflicts are so strong as to hamper markedly the candidate's psychic health. But history shows us that there have been priests and religious with some same-sex attractions who have ministered in the Church with a praiseworthy integrity. We do not want to lose these vocations.

Similarly, the other position is incomplete. The opposite position says: *There are no differences between candidates who are homosexually oriented and those who are heterosexually oriented, and we ought to treat them all the same, simply making sure that they have the capacity to live a celibate life*. This position glosses over the very real differences between these candidates. Those with homosexual attractions have unique struggles and challenges: intrapsychically, interpersonally, and pastorally. Men who present themselves as candidates with same-sex attractions ought to be screened with these struggles in mind; their formation ought to take into account their unique challenges; and the approval for their ordination ought to be particularly cognizant of the stresses and challenges that they will face as priests. In short, the bar was set too low in the past, and the priesthood and people have suffered because of it. The bar needs to be raised.

While I do not believe that the presence of any homosexual attractions should automatically exclude a candidate from priesthood, there are unique challenges and temptations for priests who have such attractions. In some places, there have been priests who have participated in a sexually active gay subculture. Obviously, such behaviors are not acceptable, morally or pastorally. In addition, the presence of such subgroups splinters the unity of priesthood and fractures its integrity. Fortunately, these groups have been the exception. It is understandable, and at times helpful, that priests who find themselves with some same-sex attractions speak to and support other priests similarly struggling with these attractions. But subgroupings of priests should always promote the wider unity of the priesthood and the integrity of its life. Presbyterates ought not to turn a blind eye to the presence of any divisive force in its midst.

Nevertheless, if one were to catalogue the sexual sins, not only of the presbyterate (which has recently been done) but also of the general population, it would be a discouraging document. All of us priests have spent more than a few hours in the confessional and in a parish office listening to story after story of such sins and failings. We quickly begin to realize how pervasively humans struggle with their sexuality. Such a powerful gift is difficult to tame. Despite the devastation that sexual failures often bring, we ought to be more compassionate with these failures, with others and with our own. This has always been one of the great gifts of Christianity, particularly our Catholic Christianity. Thank God for the cross of Christ. Thank God for the confessional. Thank God for the gift of God's mercy. Compassion is essential for the reconciled heart: compassion for victims and perpetrators, compassion for laity and bishops, compassion for those who do not think the way that we do. A lack of compassion breeds a lack of communion.

A third aspect of a reconciled heart is *seeing the complexities and nuances in life*. The opposite is being stuck in black-and-white thinking. It is common that priests who are having psychological difficulties are imprisoned behind the bars of black-and-white thinking. They are stuck in all or nothing faulty logic, excessively neat and unrealistic categories of success or failure. It is precisely such black-and-white thinking that breeds factions and diatribes.

The truth is that there are many gray areas in life. Life is not neat and clean, as we would like it. When we see the complexities of life, we realize that we do not have all the answers. As pastors, we cannot afford the luxury of living in a black-and-white world. There are too many complex situations with which our people struggle. The principles of our faith are guiding lights in a dark and difficult world. But they are not a detailed blueprint.

One dangerous new sign of black-and-white thinking that has emerged is the recent distinction between good priests and bad priests. In an otherwise laudatory effort to point out that most priests do not sexually molest minors, there has arisen the new categories of good priests and bad priests. Unfortunately, when these "bad priests" show up for a healing program, it is precisely the sense that they are innately bad that has helped to give rise to their shame-filled problems in the first place. Our splitting of people into the artificial categories of "good" and "bad" is precisely what the molester does internally. This only perpetuates a lack of integration and facing squarely one's sinfulness, either in the molester or in society as a whole. The Church has a right, and indeed an obligation, to determine fitness for ministry. Moreover, there are some criminal/sinful behaviors that can justly exclude a priest from any future ministry. But the Gospel tells us, "If we say, 'We are without sin,' we deceive ourselves, and the truth is not in us" (1 Jn 1:8). The Christian perspective is that we have all sinned.

Finally, a reconciled heart requires, of course, mature faith. If we are secure in our faith, we hold the truths steadfastly, whether convenient or inconvenient, whether approved by the public or not. When so many left Jesus because of his teaching about the Eucharist, his disciples held fast. I am encouraged by priests who have a firm commitment to teach the truth boldly. The man of communion is not a wishy-washy syncretist. He is a priest who believes strongly and passionately. As the scriptures tell us and *Dominus Jesus* affirmed, there is one Lord and one Savior and "there is no salvation through anyone else" (Acts 4:12). We believe that this Christian Church which we call Catholic is the Church founded by Christ. We believe its bishops are the direct successors of his first apostles, and the Church of Christ "continues to exist fully only in the Catholic Church."[43] Thus, our ministry of evangelization is urgent; the salvation of souls depends upon it.

At the same time, a mature faith, while passionate and convicted, is not judgmental or condemning. It is our passion and our firm belief that invites others into communion with us. A mature faith is not threatened by the beliefs of others but readily engages in a dialogue with them. This faith will not be threatened since it seeks and respects the truth, however or wherever it is found.

Some senior priests are particularly concerned today with a number of candidates to the priesthood who seem to be "rigid." It is a valid concern. "Rigidity" in this sense, is not what some would claim is merely a firm adherence to orthodoxy. In fact, it is not a question of belief at all.

Liberals and conservatives can be equally rigid. Rather, it is when a mature faith has not yet been achieved. In such cases, the faith of these men, still young in the Lord, is still somewhat fragile and they use their beliefs as weapons. Instead of engaging in dialogue, they promote diatribe; instead of promoting communion, they encourage factions to emerge. Their words are laced with anger and fear, and their actions are unconsciously violent. Their hearts are not yet reconciled.

In responding to these rigid candidates, I would, first of all, counsel patience. We cannot expect such a mature faith, or such a deeply reconciled heart, from our seminarians or even the newly ordained. All of us go through a long process of conversion, heart-softening, and developing a pastoral heart. Let us be patient with them as others were patient with us when we first engaged in the ministry.

We should also recognize that the world they are coming from is different from the world that fostered our vocations. The world of the priests and religious who are now retiring was supportive of their vocations so many years ago; the candidates of today come from a society that does not rejoice in their announcement of an interest in the priesthood. At best their desire is incomprehensible; at worst, they are the objects of derision. Thus, their entrance into the seminary is hard-won, at considerable personal expense. And they are reacting to a culture that is increasingly materialistic, narcissistic, sex-obsessed, and functionally atheistic. Their occasional rigidity is as much a necessary defense mechanism against a hostile society as it is a reflection of their own need for growth.

Nevertheless, some seminary staff often ask if such candidates should be continued in the formation process. I would answer simply by asking, "Can they be formed?"

That is, despite their rigidity, are they willing to trust you even a little and to learn and grow? If the answer is no, formation is impossible. If yes, they can become some of your very best priests.

The NFPC study on the priesthood, titled *The New Vision of Priesthood*, showed two basic types of priests in the United States today. Older priests, ordained around the time of the Second Vatican Council, emphasize flexibility, collaboration, and openness. They see the priest as a servant-leader and put great importance on calling forth the gifts of the faithful. They emphasize the centrality of baptism and their communion with the people whom they serve. On the other hand, the newly ordained priests hold to a more sacramental and cultic understanding of priesthood and see the priest as a "man set apart." They reject a theology of priesthood that is merely a matter of function. They voice a love of the Mass and a desire to enhance its beauty and transcendence. They emphasize the need for a strong prayer life and they pray the breviary regularly. They often receive the sacrament of reconciliation.[44]

Not long ago, a Vatican archbishop traveled to France. He went to a parish and was about to celebrate the Eucharist. The young curate in the parish was dressed in a clerical collar and was noted for his reverence for the Eucharist and the sacraments. He saw the archbishop, gave a cursory greeting, and abruptly left the sacristy, leaving him without assistance. The kindly pastor then emerged and entered the sacristy. He wore lay clothes and emphasized different aspects of the ministry, such as collaboration, empowerment, and pastoral sensitivity. He apologized for his curate's behavior and assisted the archbishop so that he might celebrate the Mass.

The archbishop reflected, "Wouldn't it be good to have a priest who combines both of these men?" Indeed, could we not have a priest who loves the sacraments and has a high theology of priesthood, dresses in clerical garb and is faithful to the breviary, and, at the same time, is pastorally kind and sensitive, one who empowers the laity and is among them as a servant? Are these two models mutually exclusive?

Of course, the answer is no. But it is so incredibly difficult to have a person who is both. Perhaps this is why we are ordained into a presbyterate and into a church, that is, a community of people. The Church is never Church when it is fragmented. We need priests committed to collaboration, lay ministry, and social justice. We also need priests who recognize the lofty calling of the priesthood; the priest is truly a man set apart. We need men who have a mature obedience to the faith, a joyful acceptance of our tradition, and a personal commitment to the vicar of Christ and to their bishops. At the same time, they ought to be sensitive, caring, and flexible, and be the servant who empowers others.

I suspect that we will always have individuals who have some of these gifts but not all. "Are all apostles? Are all prophets? Are all teachers? Do all work mighty deeds? Do all have gifts of healing? Do all speak in tongues? Do all interpret?" (1 Cor 12:29–30). No, the "body is one though it has many parts, and all the parts of the body, though many, are one body" (1 Cor 12:12).

In our Christian dispensation, the word "communion" carries a richness of meaning. It means that its life should ultimately center around the Eucharist, or communion, as it is popularly called. This Body of Christ is the source and the summit of that unity. It is in the Body of Christ that the many different groups, instead of breaking down into factions, are bound together into a single communion.

The priest is a man of that communion. His priesthood is devoted to the Body of Christ, inseparably tied to the Eucharist. He is to reconcile and love the many parts of the one body, the many faces that make up the church, and to shepherd them into a single whole which is Christ. "For in one Spirit we were all baptized into one body, whether Jews or Greeks, slaves or free persons, and we were all given to drink of one Spirit" (1 Cor 12:13).

Your job and mine, as priests, is to be men of communion. If the passing of this generation reveals that we have been such men and helped build a strong community of faith, then we will have done our job well.

chapter 9

The Priest Among the People: A Spirituality of Priestly Ministry[45]

When I was in the monastery, I could curb my idle talk and usually be absorbed in my prayers. Since I assumed the burden of pastoral care, my mind can no longer be collected; it is concerned with so many matters. . . . I am forced to consider the affairs of the Church. . . . I must become an administrator. . . . With my mind divided and torn to pieces by so many problems, how can I meditate or preach wholeheartedly without neglecting the ministry of the Gospel? . . . And because I too am weak . . . who am I to be a watchman, for I do not stand on the mountain of action but lie down in the valley of weakness.[46]

✣ Saint Gregory the Great

GREGORY HAD ESCHEWED HIS FORMER ADMINISTRATIVE position as prefect of Rome and devoted himself entirely to the contemplative life. When his life of prayer was threatened by his election to the papacy, he appealed unsuccessfully to Emperor Maurice not to confirm the election. But he was taken to Saint Peter's where he was consecrated the Bishop of Rome. As Pope, Gregory was a tireless worker. His deacon said that the saint never rested and worked himself tirelessly, "almost to a skeleton."

While Gregory might not be the best example of living a balanced life, his lament over losing his contemplative monastic peace and becoming weighed down with pastoral and administrative cares is one with which most priests in public ministry can readily identify. His words describe a man who believed his spiritual life had been torn to pieces once he left his monastery. Ironically, Gregory became a canonized saint and Doctor of the Church "despite" his distracted life in the world. Apparently, his own evaluation of the deteriorating quality of his spiritual life in active ministry was inaccurate.

This belief that the spiritual life of a priest engaged in ministry such as diocesan priesthood is inferior, or at least diminished because it is full of interruptions and mental burdens, endures to this day. For example, before becoming a diocesan priest, I recall being in a monastery and discussing my future with one of the monks. The monk asked what my plans were and I spoke of my intention to enter the diocesan seminary. "Oh," the monk said with a downcast look, "at least that's something."

Diocesan priesthood has long been viewed as a lifestyle with little spirituality. What spirituality it did have was thought to consist of remnants adapted from the religious life and monastic enclosures. The diocesan priest's spiritual life was thought of as being carved out of a busy day full of the demands of public ministry. Should he be called to a "higher" vocation such as the religious or monastic life, this was to be encouraged as a spiritual step up in the line of perfection. Otherwise, he remained a "secular" priest.

In current times, a conscious attempt has been made to avoid ranking vocations or orders, whether religious or lay. And since diocesan spirituality is now less frequently viewed as a remnant of the monastic life, attempts have been made to identify its unique spirituality. These efforts have suggested that our spirituality is *not* carved out of a busy day. Rather, the events of the day are an integral part of how we experience God and thus part of the very essence of our spiritual lives.

This effort at delineating a spirituality of active ministry is particularly important today. Not only is it important for the training of future diocesan clergy and for the encouragement of those who already serve in active priestly ministry, but also it is particularly urgent given the sharply declining numbers of priests available for service in the next decade.

Almost every diocese in the United States is now making plans for the future allocation of its dwindling presbyterate. For example, from 1998 to 2005, one diocese in the United States experienced a drop of over 40 percent in priests available for ministry. In 2005, there will be 40 more parishes than active priests in this diocese. Such alarming statistics are repeated in dioceses across the country and beyond.

Naturally, plans for the allocation of our scarce priests must take into account the pressing and rising ministerial needs of the community. However, such plans should also serve the goal of fostering the spiritual charism of diocesan priesthood. The danger is that future plans will ignore the diocesan charism and attempt only to fill vacant ministries.

Deployment plans will necessarily support or hinder models of diocesan priesthood depending on the principles on which they are built. It is likely that some of these plans will not state these models explicitly, but they will, nonetheless, have significant effects on the future course of priesthood in their dioceses. It is imperative that these critical plans take into account an authentic spirituality of active priestly ministry and thus the spiritual and psychological well-being of the men who serve in these vocations.

Living With the People

I would formulate what I believe to be the essence of a diocesan charism as follows: *The diocesan priest is someone who lives with the people and each becomes a part of the other's life.* Almost every other element of his spirituality flows from this one inescapable fact. We priests do not have a calling apart from the People of God whom we serve. We live among them and, as the years pass, our lives and the lives of the people whom we serve become inextricably intertwined.

This call to live among the people is not to be thought of as an abstract, transcendent concept. Rather, the diocesan priest is incardinated in a particular geographical place, his diocese, and he lives among a particular group of people. He is meant to have a special filial relationship of love and obedience for the shepherd of the diocese in which he lives. The diocesan priest may not become a mendicant, moving from place to place.

Nor may a diocesan priest live a cloistered life. A case in point is Saint Hugh who was named bishop of the See of Grenoble. Hugh was a man of great personal virtue and holiness, but also someone with considerable administrative skill. Grenoble, at the time of Saint Hugh, was noted for its corruption. He was called to leadership particularly to correct the abuses of simony, usury, and a widespread immorality in that diocese.

But Saint Hugh longed to join the monastic life. During his episcopacy he spent a considerable amount of time with Saint Bruno and the Carthusian hermits. It has been repeated for eight centuries that the founder and first prior of the Carthusians, Saint Bruno, would allow the Bishop of Grenoble to remain in solitude with the Carthusians for a short period of time. Then, with great charity and compassion, he would tell the bishop that it was time for him to leave and return to his people. As Saint Bruno knew, a diocesan priest's place is among his people, not in the charterhouse of the Carthusians.

Emotionally and Spiritually Connected

Moreover, the diocesan priest's presence among the people is not simply a physical presence. He may not remain *emotionally* and *spiritually* isolated from them.

More than a few priests fall prey to a perpetual isolation because of a lack of social skills and emotional health. While they might fulfill the bare minimum of duties necessary to remain in ministry, such as showing up for Mass and other sacramental duties, they spend the remainder of their hours in solitary pursuits.

This disconnection from the people cripples their ministry and their own psychological and spiritual health. While such priests are physically "in the world," they are not truly living a diocesan priest's vocation. They are not emotionally and spiritually "in the world."

Similarly, some deployment plans for diocesan clergy have the potential to emotionally isolate the priests from the people. An increasing number of priests will become responsible for several parishes. The danger is that these priests will become "circuit riders." They will move from parish to parish administering sacraments but may find it difficult to get to know the people or to have the people know them.

A consistent support and challenge for priests comes from the people of God. Their presence is an important way in which God is manifested to us. As we personally connect with the people whom we serve, we are affirmed, supported, challenged, and "stretched."

In, But Not of, the World

Because of his place among the people, the diocesan priest is challenged to fulfill the words of John 17: He is "in the world" but does "not belong to the world."

More than any other priest or religious, the diocesan priest is called to be "in the world." Indeed, he is a "secular" priest. But since he is firmly in the world, the danger is that he will be converted to a completely secular perspective. He is constantly tempted to lose his

Gospel vision and to become a slave of materialistic and worldly values. While accepting what is truly of value in the world around him, the priest should reject in his own life, and call to the attention of those whom he serves, those injustices and corruptions which threaten the integrity of the Christian community.

To maintain his Gospel vision in a secular world, the priest must frequently nurture this vision. There are many ways in which Gospel values are supported. For example, priests often find they are reenergized and refocused after gatherings with brother priests and others engaged in the ministry.

In addition, priests will often resort to prayer and periodic extended retreats, allowing the Spirit of God to enliven and deepen their spiritual sight. For example, they often engage in their own sort of *lectio divina*, that is, they meditate on the scriptural readings in the lectionary to prepare their weekday and Sunday homilies. This reflection time is both prayer time and preparation time. It is a good example of how diocesan priests' active ministry easily spills over into prayer.

Without a consistent resorting to these and other ways of spiritual renewal, the "priest in the world" is likely not only to become drained of his emotional and physical energy but also to lose the true reason for his vocation. A Gospel vision, like a tender shoot, must be carefully tended, particularly when it is surrounded by many forces which threaten its growth, or even its survival.

Because he is not "of" the world, the priest will not engage in every offering of society. There are a number of activities and places that inherently proclaim a set of values contrary to our own. For example, frequenting locations with bad reputations or places of great luxury would not normally be appropriate. Being in the world, the priest's actions are noticed and his life is known to his people. The priest comes to realize that how he lives his life among the people is his most important homily. The priest should maintain vigilance so that he can truly be in the world but not succumb to those worldly values that are contrary to the Gospel.

Relentless Boundary Challenges

Being in the world brings up another demanding task for the priest: establishing boundaries. Perhaps more than any other secular or religious professional, the charism of the priest sets him up for relentless assaults on his personal life and numerous challenges to his pastoral boundaries.

Secular professionals, such as lawyers or doctors, have offices set aside from their homes to serve their clients. It is almost unthinkable these days to call or meet doctors or lawyers at their private residences. There are inherent boundaries between secular professionals and their clients.

Unlike the secular professional, the diocesan priest finds his vocational calling in living with the people. The separation between what is personal and what is professional is blurred by the nature of this life. We are companions to the people. We socialize with them. We attend their parties and family functions. We meet them in the rectory as well as in their homes. We see them on the ball fields and in the schools. Our vocation calls us to be present to the people in the daily fabric of their lives. It is impossible to set up a clear boundary between our personal lives and our public ministry. Setting typical professional boundaries is not only impossible, but also it would be contrary to our charism.

There has been an increasing emphasis on the importance of boundaries for our clergy today. This is a very important and long-neglected subject. There have been, and continue to be, some very painful consequences when appropriate pastoral boundaries are crossed. However, the unique circumstances of an active priest's life pose a particularly difficult problem in maintaining these boundaries.

This challenge has become even more difficult in the post-Vatican II era. A significant shift, which has gone largely unnoticed, has taken place in diocesan ministry in the last thirty years. A powerful example of this shift is hidden within post-Vatican II liturgical changes. In the pre-Vatican II era, the priest faced away from the people; his arms were only shoulder-width apart; there was a communion rail separating him from the congregation; and he spoke in a foreign language. In liturgical as well as in a number of other pastoral settings, the boundaries were clearly set and enunciated in a number of nonverbal ways.

Now, the communion rail is gone. The priest turns and faces the people. We speak to them in their own language, the altars are moved forward, and we open our arms wide. The message has changed. Our words, the new arrangement of the sacred space, and our body language now invite the people close. They all say, "Come into my life." And they do.

People wonder why priests occasionally become over-involved with parishioners, sometimes with tragic consequences. Given the boundary changes in the modern church, I find it surprising that more do not.

I was speaking with a priest-psychologist from South America. We were talking about young priests who do not survive the first few years of ministry. We wondered together, "How can it be that a young man, who has spent more than four years preparing for a vocation, could leave the priesthood in less than a few years?" The South American priest-psychologist said that the newly ordained in his country are very quickly placed into parochial settings where they are surrounded by upwards of fifty-thousand people. He believed that these new priests are simply overwhelmed.

While most parishes do not have such enormous numbers of people, I suspect the feelings of our newly ordained are similar. It may be that some of our newly ordained are not able to establish appropriate and life-giving boundaries. If so, once the crush of ministerial demands presses upon them, they will become overwhelmed.

This feeling of being overwhelmed by the demands of the people is an increasing problem for priests in general. In the NFPC survey, the percentage of priests who cited "too much work" and the "unrealistic demands and expectations of lay people" as pressing problems has almost doubled since 1970.[47]

The diocesan priest's charism is to live among the people. This calling demands that mature boundaries be established. Yet, the nature of our ministry blurs the boundary between the pastoral and the personal and makes such a task difficult. In the post-Vatican II era, this task is all the more challenging with the erosion of many pastoral, institutional, and social boundaries that previously separated priest and people. With the rising number of Catholics, the numbers of clergy declining, and expectations increasing, the need for appropriate boundaries is all the more critical.

To protect the health of our priests, especially the newly ordained, special attention needs to be paid to the personal and pastoral boundaries of the priesthood.

Sanctifying Important Moments

In living among the people, the priest may function in a variety of roles such as counselor, administrator, civil rights advocate, or teacher, in addition to his most common role as pastor. Nevertheless, his presence in the peoples' lives always has a unique focus. His ministry ultimately points to the presence of Christ and his Gospel. As the scriptural metaphor suggests, the priest is meant to be a spiritual leaven in the whole community. He is endeavoring to be that bit of Gospel yeast that will cause the entire communal dough to rise.

Many of the faithful recognize this role of the priest. As a result, his presence is welcomed and sought out for many mundane activities. He might be asked to bless a new home or a boat about to sail. He is asked to attend picnics and athletic events. He attends public functions and, while he is often asked to perform such ordinary tasks as praying the blessing before the meal, it is really his presence that is sought. In short, the faithful are grateful for the priest's presence during the routine parts of their lives.

For many people, the priest represents the presence of Christ and his Church. They feel blessed when he is able to attend. While such appearances might be increasingly less possible with the dwindling numbers of clergy, attending public gatherings will always remain part of the priest's life as he lives out his vocation among the people. He is meant to be a spiritual leaven in the community.

But a special focus for the priest's presence is during *critical moments* in peoples' lives. A priority for the clergy has always been major events such as the birth of children, marriages, sicknesses, reconciliations, and deaths. Priests instinctively understand how important these moments are. Their presence during these critical moments is not only a consolation; priests, by virtue of their ordination and being representatives of the Church, bestow a special blessing. By the sacraments of baptism, marriage, anointing, viaticum, as well as the forgiveness of sins, he sanctifies these critical moments and raises them up to be powerful instruments of God's grace.

At times, we priests are consciously aware of the power of these moments. For example, who among us has not felt the compassionate touch of the sacrament of Reconciliation or the healing power of an anointing? While the administration of the sacraments will normally be a routine function of the priest, from time to time we experience personally their unique and saving power. As noted in Chapter Two, I believe that the priest himself, during sacramental moments, participates in the grace of Christ's presence and we receive a kind of *reflected grace*. We, too, are nourished in these moments.

A diocesan priest, as one who lives among the people, is present in the very mundane parts of human life. He is a leaven in the society, calling the people to remember that Christ is living among and in them. But in the critical moments of people's lives, the births, weddings, sicknesses, reconciliations, and deaths, he is particularly sought out. By the power of Christ in his sacraments, the priest sanctifies these moments, joining the human and divine, fusing nature and grace.

The sacramental life of the Church and the vocation of diocesan priesthood are interwoven because the lives of the people and the priest are also inextricably joined.

Standing in the Breach

As priests we spend much of our time listening to the people. After years of pastoral ministry, we become acutely aware of and sensitive to their struggles. We come to understand their hopes and dreams as well as their pains and sorrows. We empathize with them and, at times, we may even sympathize with them, that is, we may feel their pain in a personal way.

At the same time, we are initially formed and continue throughout our ministry to absorb the teachings of the Church and the radical call of the Gospel. We learn to *sentire cum ecclesia*, that is, to think with the mind of the Church. This Gospel/Church vision can present challenges to some people that are difficult for them to accept, particularly when this vision runs contrary to the secular mores of the day.

For example, in our present era, the Church's consistent and important message of respect for life is often challenged. Its teachings on the death penalty, euthanasia, contraception, and abortion are decidedly countercultural in Western society. Similarly, the Gospel call for social justice, such as an equitable sharing of the world's resources, a recognition of the most basic human rights, and a preferential option for the poor, continues to be rejected by word and deed in many of the richest and the poorest of nations. The priest stands among and with the people, appreciating their concerns and perspective, yet also exhorting and challenging them.

Because we both *empathize with people* and *think with the Church*, we may sometimes feel wedged in between some people and the teaching Church. While this may feel uncomfortable at times, it is precisely where we should be. We are the Church's representatives among the people. We also stand with and among the people; we are one of them. We are special ambassadors of Christ to his people. We are also representatives of the people before God.

It was said in the Old Testament that Moses stood in the breach between God and the people (Ps 106:23). He interceded with God for the people and he brought God's commandments, as difficult as these were, to the people. In a similar, albeit more humble way, the priest stands in the breach between God and the people. Perhaps this is why one of the most important but little recognized roles of the priest is to pray and intercede for his people.

The priest listens to and feels with the people. We think with them. We also listen to the Word of God as transmitted through the scriptures and the teachings of the Church. Thus, we take in and appropriate fully these challenging teachings. We priests stand in this mid-point. With some of the people, it becomes a point of conflict for the priest.

But a Gospel vision and Church teachings do not usually provide a strict blueprint for everyday moral decisions. The priest assists the people in interpreting these teachings for modern daily life. Our unique calling and personal understanding of the plight of the people make us particularly suited to providing pastoral guidance for the laity. In this pastoral guidance, we consistently set before the people the mercy and compassion of Jesus. Yet our pastoral sympathies should not give way to license. Sometimes the message is a difficult one.

The priest's role of standing in the breach derives directly from his charism of living among the people. Standing in the breach is an important part of the identity of a priest and, occasionally, it is our cross.

A Diocesan Celibacy

Just as the spirituality of a diocesan priest is different from his religious and monastic brothers, so his experience of celibacy is also unique. While all humans are prone to experience the pains of loneliness and, at times, feel burdened by that pain, loneliness can be a particular trial for the diocesan priest. In the NFPC survey previously cited, "loneliness" was named by diocesan priests as one of the most significant problems facing them today.[48]

Celibacy denies him the companionship of a spouse and the support of children. His charism of living among the people takes him out of the monastery and away from the support of a religious community. This charism places him, often as the only priest, alone with his people. As the numbers of clergy in some countries lessen, those who remain are increasingly separated from other priests. It is little wonder that the parish priest, after the joy of celebrating Sunday liturgies with his people, may find his spirits sinking on a Sunday afternoon when his people have all gone home to their families and he is left behind.

Diocesan priests consistently speak of the importance of the support they receive from their brother priests. Indeed, such support will be increasingly important as the numbers of priests dwindle. Groups such as *Jesu Caritas* and Emmaus can be very helpful and I recommend that they be encouraged. In my survey, it is heartening to note that 88.9 percent of priests said they have "good relationships with other priests." I believe that having good priest friends is essential for a healthy priestly life.

But the diocesan priest spends most of his time separated from other diocesan priests and immersed in his life among the people. Thus, another important support for his celibate vocation comes from the very people to whom he ministers. As celibate men, these priests often find refuge and support among a few families with whom they feel welcome and can relax. At times, such relationships can go awry in a number of ways. Nevertheless, being surrounded by the companionship of a married couple and the enthusiasm of children, even for a few hours, is a comfort.

I remember well the lament of a retiring priest. He was a particularly holy man who was much loved by his parishioners. I said to him on the eve of his retirement, "How will the people live without you?" He responded sadly, "How will I live without them?"

A Special Friend of Jesus

An active priest has a unique charism and thus a unique spiritual life. Instead of viewing his spirituality as one of trying to squeeze out a few sacred moments in an otherwise unspiritual day, he should recognize that the life of a priest among his people is an integral part of his spirituality and the way in which God is revealed to him.

At times in the past, some in diocesan ministry have misinterpreted this spirituality and have fallen prey to such rationalizations as: "My work is my prayer." While recognizing the true spirituality of public ministry, the call to prayer and to fostering a personal relationship with God is as critical for the diocesan priest as it is for those who follow any other vocation. Indeed, one can make a case for it being more important, given the pressing demands of ministry and an often hectic life of service.

Moreover, I believe an essential gift offered to the celibate priest, as noted in Chapter Four, is a unique friendship with Jesus. While this does not make the priest's vocation better than other vocations, even a cursory reading of the scriptures clearly demonstrates the special friendship Jesus had with his disciples.

Jesus personally chose twelve disciples. He called them by name. He invited them to share three precious years with him. Jesus journeyed with them. They ate together. He spoke to them plainly, as the scriptures say, and not in parables. He called them friends. And after Jesus died, his ministry was passed directly on to them.

The priest continues the ministry of Jesus in a direct and conscious way. He stands in the breach between God and the people whom he serves. With the strength provided by his unique friendship with Jesus and with the support of his people, he becomes a kind of sacrament for his people as he calls on God to sanctify their lives.

Eucharistic Summit

Ultimately, the priest's life among the people achieves its summit in the celebration of the Eucharist. It is no wonder that priests often speak of presiding at Sunday liturgy as their most fulfilling moments. The priest's greatest charism is to stand among the community around the Lord's table and to give thanks to God.

Moses stood in the breach and, raising his hands, interceded for his people. The priest, Sunday after Sunday, raises his hands in prayer and intercession. Standing with and among the people, he offers this great prayer of thanksgiving and praise. If there are sacrifices in his celibate life, and indeed there are, it is such privileged moments of grace that help sustain him through the dark hours.

The diocesan priest's particular spirituality flows from his basic call to live and grow among the people. The lives of priest and people grow together and their spiritual journeys become intertwined. This vocation has its own difficulties; it also has its moments of satisfaction and joy.

The people whom the priest serves can challenge him in many ways and, at times, they can be a cross. But more often, they are a support and a comfort. A priest who is true to his vocation will eventually see in his people a community of friends. Together, they walk the journey of life.

chapter 10

The Priest as a Grateful Person: Developing a Eucharistic Heart[49]

Love and joy are fruit of faith, sacrifice, and pain.[50]

✣ Catherine Dougherty

PRIESTS AND RELIGIOUS, WHEN THEY ARE IN DIFFICULTY AND need psychological care, enter treatment for a wide variety of psychological and spiritual illnesses. The more typical presenting issues we see are alcoholism, depression, interpersonal problems, spiritual crises, drug addictions, or destructive behaviors such as compulsive spending and credit card debt, compulsive overeating, or a variety of kinds of sexual acting out and sexual addictions.

But there are common underlying issues in their lives that give rise to these different difficulties. These underlying issues arise again and again in the course of treatment, regardless of the presenting problems. Probably the most common of them all is *anger*. When the religious and priests enter treatment, the expression on their faces is often hardened, their eyes stare straight ahead, their teeth are clenched, and their muscles tightened. Embedded deep in many of their psyches is a great deal of anger. Most of the time they are not aware of just how angry they are. I say to them, "You look a little angry." With clenched teeth and with hostility dripping from their words, the response comes back, "I am not angry!"

In itself, anger, as a human passion, is neither good nor evil. The *Catechism of the Catholic Church* tells us, "Emotions and feelings can be taken up into the virtues or perverted by the vices."[51] In this case, I am not speaking of the normal kind of anger that the healthy psyche experiences. For example, we read in Mark that Jesus looked "at them with anger and grieved at their hardness of heart . . ." (Mk 3:5). We are rightly angry at injustice and sin.

Instead, I am speaking about an entrenched anger that lodges itself in the human heart and becomes a poison that infects the entire human system. Eventually, this anger will come out in dysfunctional ways such as a serious depression in which the anger is projected inward toward the self. Or it may manifest itself in a raging personality disorder. For example, I recall a priest who terrorized the members of his parish community with his biting sarcasm, aggressive criticism and denigration of others, and his narcissistic self-aggrandizement. Such individuals have so much anger in them that when they interact with others they spread discord and conflict. Others feel hurt and upset by the manner and tone of their behavior. Priests with such anger are not "men of communion," as Pope John Paul II described. Rather, they become men of conflict and division. They leave their parishes wounded and divided.

Being filled with inner anger makes it impossible to preach truly the good news. The information and message we receive from others is much more extensive than simply interpreting the words that they speak. Much of interpersonal communication, perhaps most of it, is nonverbal. While people hear the words we speak, it is the look on our faces that they remember. I sometimes tell priests: "To check on the homily that you are really preaching Sunday after Sunday, look in the mirror." As one evangelical preacher said pointedly, "If you've been saved, please inform your face!"

At the 2002 plenary session of the Congregation for Catholic Education, John Paul II said, "It is especially necessary to foster in the students joy in their own vocation." I cannot think of a better vocational tool than a joy-filled priest. I cannot think of a better homily than a life that exudes the joy and peace that only the risen Christ can give. When we speak of the formation and ongoing formation of our priests, we are not simply teaching them information about their humanity and sexuality. Most important, we are to lead them in the very human, and very spiritual, journey out of anger into gratitude and joy. This is the nub of it: *The journey of Christian human formation is a journey out of anger into gratitude and joy.*

When we speak of priests needing to inculcate Gospel values and turn away from the ways of the "world" (a conversion of ways, as our monastic friends would call it), we include in this concept the rejection of consumerism, materialism, and a culture of death. It is important for us priests to take on Gospel values. But it is just as important for us to turn away from what underlies the world's decadence, that is, its underlying anger and inner rage. In fact, when we speak of the culture of death, we ought to include the destruction of our humanity through an inner rage and inner violence. One might say that it is this inner rage and inner violence that fuels the culture of death in our world.

It has become common to discount the role of Satan and the demonic forces in people's lives today. But I think the demonic is evident in the rage and violence that permeates this world. Satan is alive and well in the destruction of our humanity. It is not accidental that medieval depictions of demons used images of vicious animals.

A striking example of an inner violence and rage is the Gospel account of the Gerasene demoniac (cf. Mk 5:1–20). This Gospel passage displays not only striking spiritual truths, but the realistic psychology of the passage also testifies to its authenticity. The man who was possessed by legions of demons had lost his life and his humanity. He lived among the tombs, that is, he lived among the dead. He himself was spiritually and psychologically dead. Similarly, he lived away from human community; he was alone. And he was naked; only animals are naked, not human beings. He had lost his humanity and lived like an animal.

The passage goes on to say that he never rested, but day and night he screamed and gashed himself with stones. This man had no peace but was tortured within. In his pain, he screamed constantly and tried to dig out his inner pain by gashing himself. His violence was directed inward, as much of it is today, and thus his behavior was incredibly self-destructive. We see a portrait of the dying of one's humanity in isolation and inner torture. This portrait is appropriate for today. Many people today live isolated lives and are suffering intensely within. This isolation and inner pain lead them into self-destructive behavior such as alcohol, drugs, or compulsive, denigrating sex.

Having ministered in the midst of suffering religious and priests, and having walked with many on their journey of recovery, I have become a student of the transformation that occurs. They have taught me much about psychological health. Even more strikingly, they have taught me much about the good news of Jesus. I remember one resident who finished our program only a short time ago. We typically have a final departure liturgy before the resident returns home. At this liturgy, the priest-resident was invited to give a reflection to the entire community. He stood up and said, "When I first came to Saint Luke Institute, I believed that I was sent here because the bishop and his vicars hated me. About halfway through the program, I changed my understanding and believed that I had been sentenced to Saint Luke's because God was punishing me for my sins. As I now finish the program, I have come to realize that I have been here because God loves me and because my bishop cares about me. They wanted me to get better. Being here has been one of the greatest graces of my life."

His journey from anger and bitterness to gratitude was stunning. In reality, we see this transformation over and over again. Residents often begin their journey filled with rage and fear. If the process is successful, they will undergo a transformation that ends in gratitude and inner peace. This is a wonderful marker to help assess whether the therapy has been successful. If the resident stays stuck in much anger and continues to see himself as a helpless victim, there is a great deal more work to be done. But if we see on his face a sense of peace and gratitude, then we know that the transformation has taken hold.

Similarly, could one not say that the good news had taken hold as well? It would not be a stretch to say that the transformation of the human spirit from anger and fear to gratitude and joy is not only the soul of human formation, it is the stuff of a Christian conversion as well.

Nevertheless, it is helpful to separate cognitively what is psychological and what is spiritual. One danger of our times is to collapse everything spiritual into the psychological, thus all spirituality becomes clothed in psychological language. In this fallacy, psychotherapy replaces spiritual direction and John of the Cross is replaced by Carl Jung. But human formation is not an end in itself. It should eventually open us up to what is authentically spiritual, the infinite divine, and thus we transcend the limitations of our frail humanity.

The opposite error is equally dangerous, that is, denying what is human and casting everything in spiritual language. Unfortunately, many of the priests and religious in difficulty have done just that. They speak eloquently about the spiritual journey but their words are not rooted in their personal lives. In reality, their spiritual lives are empty. Sadly, we have seen the devastation to the Church and society when the human formation of our priests is lacking.

But, in the end, the spiritual and the psychological are so intertwined in the human person that they are inseparable. It reminds me of the title of one of Jacques Maritain's greatest works, *The Degrees of Knowledge: Distinguish to Unite*. While we can distinguish the difference between the psyche and the spirit, we do so only to unite them in the end. In our work of healing, it is impossible to delineate clearly where the psychological ends and the spiritual begins. This spiritual and psychological journey is one human pilgrimage.

The Psychology of Gratitude

It seems to me that this healing transformation, which is so central to the therapeutic journey, is an apt description of human formation as well. In reality, the therapeutic work that we do at Saint Luke Institute is simply a microcosm of the human journey and, I believe, a program in Christian conversion as well.

There is an increasing amount of psychological research on the subject of gratitude. I have been impressed with the work of Michael McCullough, Ph.D., and Robert Emmons, Ph.D. They have found that those who practiced being grateful, such as keeping a daily journal of what they were grateful for, were measurably better off physically, psychologically, and spiritually, especially when compared to those who kept a list of daily hassles and irritants. (Don't we all have a tendency to focus on the negative events of the day rather than the positive!)

Physically, the gratitude group exercised more, had fewer physical symptoms, and slept better. Psychologically, they reported higher levels of alertness, enthusiasm, determination, and energy. They experienced less depression and stress as well as high levels of optimism and life satisfaction, without denying the negative aspects of their lives. Spiritually, they were more likely to help others, they were less envious of others, less materialistic, more generous, and more likely to attend religious services and engage in religious activities. Clearly, being grateful is good for you![52]

The Christian Spirituality of Gratitude

Being grateful is not only good for you, it is, not accidentally, integral to the Christian life. In fact, one could say categorically that the person who is not grateful is not a Christian.

We read in 1 Thessalonians that giving thanks is a work in which the Christian should always be engaged. "Rejoice always. Pray without ceasing. In all circumstances give thanks, for this is the will of God for you" (5:16–18). Similarly, the Letter to the Colossians says: "Be thankful. Let the word of Christ dwell in you richly, as in all wisdom you teach and admonish one another, singing psalms, hymns, and spiritual songs with gratitude in your hearts to God. And whatever you do . . . do everything in the name of the Lord Jesus, giving thanks to God the Father through him" (3:15–17). Thanksgiving is a foundational attitude and work of the Christian.

The New Testament even suggests that those who do not give thanks are not saved. The *acharistoi* are those who are ungrateful and they are rejected (2 Tm 3:2) while the *eucharistoi* give thanks and are saved (Col 3:15). In the light of these reflections, the Preface to Eucharistic Prayer II now makes much theological sense: "Father, it is our duty and our salvation always and everywhere to give you thanks." We, as Christians, not only give thanks to God as it is fitting for us to do, but it is also our *salvation*. These are stunning words: It is our salvation to give thanks!

The Mass itself, the source and summit of the Christian life, is properly called the Eucharist. As the Greek *eucharistia* denotes, we give thanks to God. We know that the gift of God is made "effective and present ... it is actualized and objectified" in us as we participate in this eucharistic act of giving thanks.[53] In this act of giving thanks, we are taken up into the mystery of Christ's redemption and participate in the salvation he won for us. *To give thanks is to be a Christian and it is to be saved.*

I have always loved the account of the cleansing of the ten lepers (cf. Lk 17:11–19). I believe that the Gospel passage is often underinterpreted. I think we miss its power and profundity. The account could be interpreted as a kind of summation of the good news. Jesus heals ten people, ten lepers, but only one of them returns. We might think to ourselves, "It is too bad that only one of them had the courtesy to return and give thanks." But this would be to miss the critical interaction between the healed Samaritan who returned and Jesus. When he does return, he does not extend a handshake in gratitude. Rather, he falls on his face and praises God. In Old Testament times, people fell on their faces in the midst of a theophany, that is, when God revealed himself. This one leper realized, that not only had he been healed, but also it was God who had done it. He fell on his face at the feet of Jesus, and gave thanks and praise to God. Jesus then pronounced a word of salvation, "Go your way, your faith has saved you." It was in the very act of recognizing what God in Jesus had done for him, and giving thanks, that this man was saved. As it says in the preface to Eucharistic Prayer II, "Father, it is our duty *and our salvation*, always and everywhere to give you thanks."

If we are to become true priests, then we must become eucharistic people, that is, we become men who are grateful and live lives of gratitude. It is a terrible disjunction to preside at the Eucharist and to be someone without a grateful heart. To be a priest fully is to be a grateful person.

A Psychological Paschal Mystery

How do we make this saving journey from anger to gratitude? I have watched our residents at Saint Luke Institute and their experiences have taught me something about the journey of human formation. Being in the Institute, one senses much joy, but there is also much pain. I typically ask priests at the end of their stay how their time in treatment went. Many priests say to me, "It saved my life." When I ask them if it was difficult, they often roll their eyes and say it was incredibly difficult. Day after day they had to face the pains and hurts of their lives. Day after day they struggled through much inner conflict and went into places psychologically that they never would have chosen to go.

This healing journey is a kind of paschal mystery. One might call it a psychological paschal mystery. Before we come to the "resurrection" of the psyche, we must first descend into the cross of one's difficulties and pains. Before one can know gratitude and peace, one descends first into the anger and hurt that lie buried and are poisoning the spirit. As Catherine Doherty wrote, "Love and joy are fruits of faith, sacrifice, and pain."

It reminds me of the work of Walter Brueggemann titled *The Message of the Psalms*. Brueggemann noted that there are many psalms that he called the "psalms of disorientation" or "psalms of darkness." Here, the psalmist is in distress and prays honestly and directly to God. One hears in these psalms much hurt, pain, and, at times, anger. Brueggemann explains why these prayers of Israel were so honest in their address to God:

> The presupposition and affirmation of these psalms is that precisely in such deathly places as presented in these psalms new life is given by God. . . . It embraces darkness as the very stuff of new life. Indeed, Israel seems to know that new life comes nowhere else.[54]

It is noteworthy that the psalms now comprise the bulk of the official prayers of the Church, and thus the Liturgy of the Hours that we priests pray daily.When priests and religious come to Saint Luke Institute, their spiritual lives often have become disconnected from their real lives. In order to reconnect them, we ask them to sit in the chapel, at least twenty to thirty minutes each day, and open their hearts and let God know what is going on in their lives, especially any feelings of fear, anger, or distress. "Be honest with yourself and with God," we tell them. Our clients, in order to enter a transformation of heart, must open their hearts to God. Also, they must descend into the very darkness of their lives in order to find new life or, as Brueggemann says, new life comes from descending into the deathly places of our lives and presenting them to God.

While most priests do not undergo a formal therapeutic program like Saint Luke's, the same principles of human formation apply to both. We priests must be able to "descend into the deathly places" of our lives, and thus be able to journey with the people as they descend into the darkness of their own lives.

Courage, Honesty, and Trust

Praying these psalms of darkness suggests the presence of some important qualities which are essential to develop in any process of human formation. To navigate this psychological paschal mystery implies, first of all, *courage*. Such a journey is not for the faint of heart. It requires *honesty* with oneself, a willingness to face the truth. Most of all, it suggests a growing *trust*. Seminarians need to be formed into developing enough of a trust in the formation staff to speak honestly of their lives and struggles. These qualities are important for a future healthy life as a priest and they are often lacking in the priests and religious in difficulty. As they are developed, much healing takes place.

As noted in Chapter Eight, there has been much said these days about the presence of some seminarians and priests who are called "rigid." Many times people will ask mental health professionals about such individuals. What is their problem? What should we do? I am not speaking of a person who has a strong faith and speaks this faith with directness and honesty. Second, I am not speaking of a specific theological bent because rigid people can come in all walks of life: liberal or conservative, young or old. Rather, rigidity is a mask for much fear and distrust. The inner self is still very fragile and the person protects this fragile self by not listening to others and fanatically clinging to inner platitudes and simplistic modes of thought. In its most extreme forms, there is no growth possible because the individual will not take in any ideas that do not conform to his own inflexible pattern, and thus, there is no possibility of change.

What drives this stance is fear. Therefore, in the process of formation or healing, the rigid person ought to be approached slowly and in a nonthreatening way. A direct confrontation with the person is likely to be counterproductive; it only elevates his fear and increases the strength of his psychological defenses. Rather, the approach should be to foster a good relationship with the individual, slowly letting his fears subside and a relationship of trust to develop. In the very process of building trust and assuaging fear, the person makes a strong step forward in human formation. Building trust and reducing fear are themselves part of the process of human formation. Not surprisingly, much of the stuck anger in our world is a combination of anger and fear.

In *Pastores Dabo Vobis*, John Paul II delineated some qualities that comprise authentic human formation. He spoke of the need for a "capacity to relate to others" and the need for "true friendship." *I could not support these more strongly.* They are, indeed, essentials in human formation. Building relationships requires trust and honesty, necessary elements in the process of human formation. And the presence of solid peer relationships is one of the best indicators of a healthy psyche.

Another common underlying theme of the priests and religious who come to us is the lack of peer relationships. Fortunately, in the process of human formation and re-formation, people can learn how to make friends. This is true for the seventy-year-old as well as the twenty-year-old. Building friendships is a social skill that can be developed.

After the Gerasene demoniac encounters Jesus, the demons are cast out and he is transformed. He is no longer naked but fully clothed, that is, he is no longer an animal. He "sits," that is, he can rest; he has inner peace. He is no longer tortured inside. He no longer will live among the dead but now wants to accompany Jesus. He wants to reenter the world of human beings. He is fully human once again. It is in our encounter with Jesus that we become fully human. It is in Jesus that our humanity is finally and completely formed.

Do Not Be Afraid

My days at Saint Luke Institute have convinced me of how destructive fear can be. Fear paralyzes the psyche. It stops us from trusting others. It destroys human relationships. It keeps us from looking inside ourselves and descending into the darkness within. Thus, it keeps us from embarking on the road to human transformation.

It is surprising how many times Jesus encourages us with the words, "Do not be afraid." He rarely spoke about sexual sins. But he often spoke to us about fear. Sexual sins can cause much scandal and devastation; however, fear destroys the very ground of faith, trust in God.

I think it providential that John Paul II began his pontificate from the balcony at Saint Peter's with the inspired words, "Do not be afraid." These are important words given to us by our Savior. They are important words for the Church. They are important for our priests. Do not be afraid. It is fear that paralyzes the psyche. It is fear that kills relationships. It is fear that keeps us from embracing the cross of suffering which, in faith, leads us to a resurrection of gratitude and joy. I wish there was an easier way. Sometimes I say to our residents, "I wish that the program here was easier; I wish that you did not have to undergo such a painful transformation." But, sadly, there is no shortcut; there is no easy path.

The road to becoming fully alive and fully human is a long one that continues in earnest after ordination. We continue to experience a kind of paschal mystery by diving into the darkness of our lives, and the darkness of the lives of those to whom we minister, and we eventually experience a birth to new life. We feel the hurt, anger, pain, and sorrow buried in the fallen human heart so that we might nurture the gratitude of the Christian and the joy of the risen Christ.

In the end, human transformation is the process whereby we become a eucharistic people. Our spirits soar with an authentic gratitude for all that God has done. The joy of the risen Christ suffuses our hearts and shines through our faces and lives. Getting to such a place is long and painful. But, it is a journey well worth taking.

chapter 11

When Things Go Wrong

One of the brethren had sinned, and the priest told him to leave the community. So then [the elder] Abbot Bessarion got up and walked out with him, saying: "I too am a sinner!"[55]

✣ THOMAS MERTON

I WOULD BE REMISS IF I DID NOT DEVOTE A SEPARATE CHAPTER to priests in difficulty. I have spent the last 15 years working with priests who find themselves with serious problems. I believe it is important for me to take a moment and to address a few words to them.

My first thought is that the priests and religious women and men who find themselves with serious problems are especially beloved. I believe that God has a special solicitude for priests and religious in distress. They have served God and the people for many years and assisted many in need; now it is time for them to receive help. Perhaps at such a moment, contrary to their expectation, they have become the littlest of all and thus more closely conformed to Christ than at any other time in their lives. When we are the smallest and most in need, the divine compassion overflows most powerfully. "For the kingdom of God belongs to such as these" (Lk 18:16).

Priests have problems not because they are priests, but because they are human. One time I received a phone call from a television producer. He said he was going to do a television show on depression in the priesthood. He wanted to investigate the widespread depression in the priesthood and try to determine its causes. He wanted me to help with this television show. My response was, "Let's start with your basic assumption. You are assuming that priests are more likely to be depressed than others. What makes you believe that?" He hemmed and hawed a while, mumbling something a bit incoherent. I responded by saying, "It is true that some priests are depressed. But my impression is priests are no more likely to be depressed than anyone else. In fact, the rate of depression in the priesthood is probably lower than the general population." I never heard anything more about the television show.

In fact, if one looks at my survey responses, they would suggest that depression in the priesthood is very low. It is well nigh impossible to be seriously depressed and at the same time love what you are doing, find great satisfaction in it, and report that you are contented and fulfilled. In my survey, I asked the respondents directly if they felt depressed. A small percentage, only 3.2 percent, said they felt depressed all or most of the time. Given the beating that our priests have taken recently, their emotional resilience is inspiring.

Overall, my impression is that psychopathology, that is, serious psychological problems, do indeed manifest themselves in the priesthood, but probably at no higher a rate than the general population. Given the in-depth psychological screening that just about every diocese and religious has had for its priests during the last twenty years or more, much of the very debilitating psychopathology is screened out. For example, it is unusual for a priest to be schizophrenic, floridly psychotic, or to suffer from a serious bipolar illness. Most of these major pathologies are screened out before ordination. Of course, lesser pathologies may make it through the process, and pathology can greatly exacerbate or even begin after ordination, thus making initial screening ineffective. Nonetheless, the screening and long formation process do provide some safeguards against seriously mentally ill individuals becoming priests.

Shame in Needing Psychological Care

Occasionally, however, psychological problems do manifest themselves in our priests. It is a distressing problem. In 1992 I conducted a survey of 1,013 active lay Catholics from the United States and Canada. These are people who know priests personally and work closely with them. The lay respondents were given the statement, "I expect a priest's conduct to be better than other people's conduct." A large majority, 83 percent, agreed.[56] While people intellectually recognize that priests are human beings and thus have human problems, they still have difficulty accepting the reality.

It is interesting that there was one group who had the very highest expectations of priests. Eighty-seven percent of this sample endorsed the statement that a priest's moral conduct should be better than others. This group was priests themselves.[57] Priests have the highest expectations of their own conduct and they are the most crestfallen when priests do not measure up to their own high expectations, especially when that person happens to be oneself.

This is clearly manifested when a priest enters psychological treatment. While most people feel ashamed when they need psychological care, priests feel doubly shamed. It is a major issue to confront in the beginning of treatment.

It is no surprise that priests are unlikely to seek treatment of their own accord. Given the shame they feel and also given that they view themselves as caregivers, not caregetters, they are unlikely to ask for help. Some do. The large majority do not. And even when they enter a healing regimen, it can be a difficult transition to allow themselves to be cared for. They have to learn a whole new way of practicing humility. This is not the humility of the priest washing the people's feet during Holy Thursday liturgy. It is the humility of taking off your shoes and allowing someone *else* to wash *your* feet. This takes its own kind of humility. It is good for us priests to learn to be grateful for receiving help.

Typical Presenting Problems

While priests can and do suffer from just about every human problem, there is a common list of significant problems that surface with some regularity. These are the presenting issues or typical reasons why a priest will be referred for psychological assistance. This list, in no particular order, includes such problems as: alcohol and drug abuse, depression, a variety of kinds of sexual acting out, cyber-sex, anxiety, compulsive eating, mismanagement of money, and several kinds of personality disorders including narcissism and dependent personalities.

A few priests, but not many, are drug abusers. Occasionally they will be involved with marijuana and some with cocaine. I strongly urge every priest, and everyone in general, not to become involved with cocaine. There is a fairly high rate of treatment failure (early relapse) with cocaine addictions. Sustained use actually changes brain chemistry. It is a terrible addiction to overcome. Avoid it at all costs!

More priests are alcohol abusers. While society has become more knowledgeable about alcohol abuse, it remains a common problem. Most priest alcoholics are not "falling down drunks," rather they are functional alcoholics who use alcohol as a way of dealing with a whole host of problems. Once the priest stops drinking, then the real therapy can begin. Why do you drink? Let us help you deal with your challenges in a healthier way.

While it seems that some alcoholics have simply inherited an alcoholism gene through family transmission, many use alcohol as a way of dealing with inner anxiety and/or depression, inner conflicts (such as sexual desires that they dislike) or with external conflicts, anger and disappointment. These priests need to learn how to face such problems without resorting to alcohol.

Depression in alcoholics is not uncommon. For example, the alcoholic may try to medicate depression with alcohol and conversely alcohol can eventually exacerbate an underlying depression. Alcohol and depression are a nasty combination.

There are many kinds of depression. Some priests suffer from major depressions and may go through an intense period of depression in which they find it difficult to function. However, most priests who are depressed have a milder form of depression which is a chronic, low level, depressive effect called dysthymia. I suggest to priests that they look in the mirror. I say, "If you haven't smiled in the past couple of months, something is wrong." Those with dysthymia are often so accustomed to being depressed that they are not even aware of it. Many of them do not remember, if they ever knew, what it was like to feel good. Fortunately, the large majority of depressions can be ameliorated as a result of treatment.

I have psychologically evaluated many a priest caught in a long-term, chronic, mild depression, that is, dysthymia. Some spiritualize their condition, thinking that this dour mood is a sign of their sanctity. It is true that those who suffer from psychological illnesses, if they bear them in faith, can become holy through their long suffering. However, many times their depression is treatable. As I tell them, "It's not a sin to be happy." In fact, as we shall see in the final chapter, an abiding sense of joy is a sign of the indwelling of the Holy Spirit.

Personality Disorders in the Priesthood

More than a few priests who are referred to psychological treatment suffer from personality disorders, that is, a chronic, long-term, maladaptive way of relating to others. This results in dysfunctional interpersonal relationships. Typically, such priests have interpersonal problems wherever they go. They simply have a dysfunctional way of relating to others and no matter what milieu they are placed in, they carry the problem with them.

An inherent difficulty is that the person does not see the disorder himself. Someone with a personality disorder lives within his distorted perception of others and self and, thus, cannot "see" the problem. The person may be aware of the conflicts and problems that surface because of the disorder, but he will ascribe the problems to others. The individual will blame the people, another priest, the bishop, or anyone else, but he will not point to himself.

There are many different kinds of personality disorders. One major type is *narcissism*. The narcissist is the person whose major focus is himself. He needs adulation and support from others. He cannot handle criticism. He is often charming and kind, until he is crossed. Then his inner rage, long buried within, comes out in a torrent. The narcissist believes he is special and should be treated as such. He lacks empathy for others and tends to use others for his own self-aggrandizement. The priest narcissist often has a following of individuals who are his "groupies." The worst thing to do is to put a narcissist in charge.

On the other hand, the *dependent* personality has difficulty expressing himself and his own opinion. He wants others to make the decisions and he is not assertive. He does not want to disagree with others for fear of rejection or disapproval. Dependent individuals go to excessive lengths to be liked and to receive approval from others. They lack self-confidence and independence.

Some priests are *passive-aggressive*, that is, they seem agreeable on the outside, but subtly undermine others, especially leaders. They appear to be obedient, but there is a pervasive pattern of passive resistance and negativism. Such individuals often feel cheated, unappreciated, and misunderstood. They chronically complain to others. They are the bane of every bishop.

There are other priests who are just plain difficult. They are negative, chronic complainers, and pervasively angry. While this is not an official diagnosis in the psychiatric manual, I would describe them as having "resistant" or "angry" personality disorders. They erupt into fits of anger with others and consistently frustrate parishioners. They can be a bit paranoid and think that others are out to do them harm. They have an underlying fear, anger, and unhappiness that poison their lives and their parishes.

There are many other kinds of personality disorders, but the aforementioned are the most common among priests. Typically, these priests go from parish to parish, creating as many problems as they solve. One typical sign of a personality disordered priest is that the parish becomes divided. Instead of being a man of communion, he is a man of division. Instead of building community, he tears it down. Eventually, the personnel office in the chancery or religious order has no place to assign him because no one will take him.

This is a sad situation. Personality disorders are hard to treat psychologically and tend to be long-lasting.

Typically, the goal is to contain not cure. Such individuals may respond to treatment if they are willing to try. Most priests with personality disorders can learn to function adequately but need supervision and clear limits. If they cross the limits and act inappropriately, they need to be reprimanded and disciplined.

However, priests with personality disorders should not be placed in positions of significant authority. They are not usually able to be pastors. The worst thing for an organization is to have a leader with a personality disorder. Satan, I am convinced, is one massive personality disorder and hell is a very dysfunctional place indeed!

I would add this word to my brothers. If you find yourself having chronic interpersonal problems and you are willing to face the issues courageously, then considerable help and healing is available. The power of the Gospel is unlimited; we only need to cooperate with it. But the personality disordered priest needs to be willing to listen to others and to take into his heart what is said. He cannot be a slave to his own "self-will run riot." Trust in the perception of others is key to making changes in one's life.

Sexual Misconduct in the Clergy

We are all aware of problems with priests acting out sexually. These are the stories that hit the front page. It is big news when a celibate priest gets caught in some sexual behavior, particularly if the act is illegal. The sensational aspect of such a story is too hot for the media to pass up. Such stories have strong shock value and they are subtly titillating to the reader.

As a result, a disproportionate amount of media attention is focused on priests engaged in sexual misconduct with the resulting impression that priests are uniquely dysfunctional. I recall being on a CNN show and the anchor mentioned that they had just completed a poll which indicated that over 60 percent of Americans believed that child sexual abuse was very frequent or somewhat frequent among Catholic priests. The anchor himself realized that this was an exaggeration. He suggested that the reason for this distorted perception was the blanket media coverage of the problem, which gave people a false impression.

Sexual misconduct among Catholic priests is scandalous. One case is one too many. It causes untold harm to victims and their families, to the Church, and to the priest himself. But there are no data to support the idea that Catholic priests have any more sexual difficulties than other adult men. Nevertheless, we do expect them to be better and we are shocked when they are not, particularly if their problem is sexual.

One person who is very upset by the problem and full of shame, as previously noted, is the priest himself. Many priests will enter treatment feeling like "walking shame." They will say things like: "There is no hope for me," or "Everything I have done is a lie," or "If people really knew me, they would know that I am a fraud." In the beginning, some feel so despicable they cannot even attend Mass. This despair, self-denigration, and pervasive shame are part of their disorders and need to be addressed in the healing process.

Eventually the priest needs to realize that he is a good person, created in God's image, and has done many good things as a priest. However, he has a serious problem that has harmed others and needs to address it directly, for the good of all, including himself.

Some want to label these priests as bad and not like us. They want to brand them for their infidelity and place them in a separate category, like the unclean lepers of Israel who were isolated from society and walked ringing a bell, shouting, "Unclean, unclean!" This is psychologically dangerous. The more we isolate and stigmatize such people, the more likely they are to act out their problems. They are safest when they are treated, given some sort of productive work, and are supervised. They ought to be kept away from areas of temptation. For example, alcoholics ought not to work in liquor stores; men who have preyed on women should not supervise or minister individually and directly to women; and those who have molested minors should be kept away from direct, unsupervised contact with children.

Regardless of the kinds of sexual problems some priests have, I say to our priests most clearly, "You cannot live a double life. You cannot continue to engage in sexual behaviors and live priesthood. Whatever your sexual problems and challenges, they can and must be dealt with directly. You can and must live a celibate life. Perhaps you do not believe it now, but trust me; many others have had similar problems and they have found hope and healing. The vast majority has gone on to lead lives of integrity. You can, too, and you will be glad that you did."

Underlying Issues

These typical presenting problems, substance abuse, depression, a variety of kinds of sexual acting out, cybersex, anxiety, compulsive eating, mismanagement of money, and several kinds of personality disorders, are only presenting issues. That is, they are the external symptoms of underlying issues that need to be addressed. After dealing with many priests with such problems, a number of common underlying problems keep surfacing. These underlying issues either give rise to the presenting problems in the first place, exacerbate them, or, at a minimum, sustain their existence. If the underlying issues are addressed, the presenting problems will either disappear altogether or become much more manageable.

Two of these underlying issues have already been mentioned in previous chapters: *anger* and *lack of peer relationships*. There is much buried anger that is the fuel that keeps alive many of these problems. Cut off the fuel supply and the dysfunction will disappear. Heal the anger and the bitter priest can become a man of communion and peace.

Tied to the anger is isolation and a lack of peer relationships. Many of our priests have hundreds of acquaintances but no real friends. As noted in a previous chapter, the priest may know a lot of people but the relationships are superficial. He does not share his inner self and, as a result, others know little about him. There is no one to hear the hurt in his life and the disappointments. There is no one to support him when he is down. It is true that he is celibate. But, unfortunately, he is more than celibate. He is alone. Celibacy cannot be lived well without real friends.

There are other underlying issues that give rise to the presenting problems which priests have. Many carry a variety of *unhealed hurts and traumas from childhood*. Some grew up in alcoholic homes or were sexually or physically abused. Others grew up not feeling accepted or worthwhile. Some came from broken homes and became the caretakers for their younger siblings or for their divorced mothers. More than a few have not come to terms with their sexual feelings and associate much guilt and shame with them.

Sometimes people wonder why a particular priest is so dysfunctional. But after doing a psychological assessment and learning what is buried behind his poor behavior, I wonder how he is functioning at all. Given the severe trauma that some have suffered as children, it is a miracle that they are not in a locked psychiatric asylum.

Nevertheless, such childhood traumas can be healed. Through prayer, the sacraments, and psychotherapy, if needed, such traumas can be largely put to rest. While healing processes do not take the past away, they help the individual to live in peace, no longer tormented or whipsawed by the past. The past does not go away, but it loses its power to make us miserable and control our lives.

Closely connected to childhood traumas is the common underlying issue of a *negative self-image*. Psychology often raises up this concept of self-image, at times, perhaps excessively so. But the fact is, when our self-perception is damaged, there are all sorts of problems that surface such as scrupulosity, depression, anxiety, self-mutilation, and eating disorders. While each of these is a complex phenomenon, a damaged self-image fuels psychopathology.

Some therapists recommend looking into the mirror and repeating positive statements about oneself. This can be helpful, but there is no substitute for feeling the love and acceptance of others, and the love and acceptance of God. Realizing that we are loved, just as we are, facilitates incredible healing. *The Christian message of God's steadfast love for us is the most healing of all therapies.*

Finally, I would add one more frequent, underlying issue that gives rise to common psychological problems in our priests. It is a *fractured or nonexistent spiritual life*. As mentioned earlier, Twelve Step lore tells us: "Spirituality is the first thing to go and the last thing to return." It is sad that a few of our priests have stopped living any meaningful spiritual life. Celibacy makes no sense without a vibrant relationship to God. Priesthood is empty without daily opening ourselves up to God's powerful presence. There is little hope for a priest's mental health if he does not pray. Spirituality is good for us on all levels, including the physical and the psychological. And a quick ticket to a dysfunctional life for a priest is to stop praying. Serious problems are not far behind.

What often happens is that the priest, who has stopped living any meaningful spiritual life, or perhaps never started, is caught up in a superficial spiritual life that he confuses for real depth. He will speak eloquently using theological and spiritual phrases that he has read and heard, but they will not have any personal substance. Often, the spirituality of priests in difficulty is excessively intellectualized and rationalized. They know the right words, but they ring hollow in their own lives.

Preventing Problems Before They Occur

I am often asked to come to a diocese and speak to the presbyterate about living a healthy life. I am glad to do so and I think it is important. It shows a real commitment on the part of the priests and bishop to help the priests live lives of integrity and wholeness.

However, simply coming to a diocese and telling the priests all the behaviors they are not supposed to engage in is limited at best and likely to be ineffective. The priests already know they are not supposed to become alcoholics or steal money. They know they are not supposed to have sexual relations or view pornography on the Internet. They know that drug abuse is wrong. A program in wellness does not only set out the "nos." More important, it needs to address the underlying issues that give rise to the behaviors in the first place.

As noted above, when priests are beset with unaddressed childhood trauma, when they are isolated and angry, when they have a damaged self-image and their spiritual lives are empty, they are not far from a personal melt-down. The manner in which these underlying problems will finally be manifest depends upon the predispositions of each priest, but they *will* come out and in very negative ways.

What is the answer? The answer is both individual and collective. Individually, such priests need to enter a personal helping relationship, perhaps more than one. Some believe that spiritual direction is sufficient. At times, it is. However, it is just as likely that the priest who excessively intellectualizes his spiritual life will try to use spiritual direction as just another defense against truly facing his problems. I have known more than one priest who conned his bishop into not requesting that the priest go into psychological treatment by saying that spiritual direction would address his sexual compulsivity. It is little surprise that it rarely does. Spiritual direction is very important, but it is not appropriate for the treatment of major psychological problems. Thus, priests in difficulty will want to find assistance on a variety of levels—spiritual, psychological, and perhaps physical.

But the answer is a collective one as well. The more we foster presbyterates and dioceses that are places of true communion, the more healing and life-giving they will be. Healthy presbyterates, promoting mutual support and a positive unity, will bolster the well-being of individual priests. Making time and space plus devoting resources to clergy convocations, priestly days of reflection, training spiritual directors for priests, sabbaticals, and priest support groups are all time and money well spent. Bishops and clergy personnel directors would do well to attend to and foster the health of their entire presbyterates, in addition to their all too consuming work with a few priests in difficulty. Wellness is both a collective and an individual reality.

Fundamental Human Challenges

Underneath the aforementioned problems is an even deeper substrata of human challenges. I have watched the journey of recovery for many priests and religious women and men. As they struggled to find healing and life, I witnessed a basic level of human struggle that seems common to all people. Indeed, their healing journey is only a microcosm of essential human challenges.

The challenges of this fundamental substrata might be put forward as:

- *Resting in an Inner Peace versus Torn by Inner Conflict and Violence*
- *Finding Gratitude versus Stuck in Anger*
- *Connecting in Intimacy versus Living in Isolation*
- *Rising to Hope versus Sinking in Despair*

These are some of the ultimate challenges of life. They describe the attributes of the next life, which bring to their fullness the choices we have made. We rise to the heaven of peace, gratitude, intimacy, and hope; or we find ourselves in the hell of violence, conflict, anger, isolation, and despair.

No one can make us choose one or the other. We are not determinists but rejoice in the gift of human freedom. It is our God-given power to choose heaven or hell. And choose we must. In the end, we find one or the other. But the good news is that it takes only a drop of heaven to vanquish hell. We do not need to be full of hope; we only need a glimmer. We do not need to be perfectly grateful or to be perfectly at peace; we only need to have a sliver of God's peace in our heart and to form the words on our lips, "Thank you, God," in order to be saved.

The Grace of Alcoholism

The journey to a heaven of hope, intimacy, gratitude, and peace is not a steady rising up to the heavens. Rather, it is a paschal mystery that requires us first to be brought low. As Christ, we "descend into hell" so that we might be raised to life.

More than one priest-alcoholic in recovery has said to me, "I thank God for the gift of my alcoholism." Needless to say, the first couple of times I heard it, I was confused as to what they meant. As they explained it to me, it made much Christian sense. They invariably meant that their alcoholism brought them to their knees. It was in this pathology that they came to realize that they needed God. Without it, they would have continued to believe they could go it alone.

The first two steps of the Twelve Steps of AA capture this insight well. The alcoholic must admit that his/her life is out of control and that only God has the power to help the person to sobriety. The alcoholic does not find sobriety by force of personal will, but rather through a complete, and initially scary, surrender to God. These alcoholics realized that without this disease they never would have totally surrendered themselves to God. Priests with other problems, including sexual ones, have told me the same thing. It was their disorder and their problems that led them into the arms of God.

We ought to be remorseful for the harm and pain we have caused to others. We do not rejoice in broken humanity. But we do rejoice in our God who brings life out of death, and light out of darkness. When we are brought low, we are most receptive to the good news of Jesus. Perhaps we ought not to ostracize priests, or others, with problems. Rather, we might see in them the suffering face of Christ and the possibility that they could become living witnesses to new life. Perhaps they can be some of our best priests because they have truly lived the paschal mystery. It is as many priests have told me as they completed the healing program, "I feel like I am ready to be a priest for the first time."

chapter 12

Renewal of the Priesthood[58]

This time of trial will bring a purification of the entire Catholic community, a purification that is urgently needed.[59]

✠ John Paul II

IN HIS OPENING ADDRESS AT THE 2002 BISHOPS' CONFERENCE in Dallas, USCCB president Bishop Wilton Gregory praised the media for helping the victims of child sexual abuse to come forward. But he went on in his remarks to criticize its coverage of the Church which "has been distorted to an extent which I would not have thought possible six months ago." It was not only Church officials who felt the media coverage distorted the truth. The *New York Times* religion editor Peter Steinfels wrote in the *Tablet*:

> After months of media blitz most Americans, including normally well-informed Catholics, have a skewed understanding of the clerical sex scandal... of its exact scope, the time frame when it largely occurred, the legal issues involved, and the record of how different bishops handled it at different times.[60]

There was truth to the media's basic story. Some Catholic priests had sexually molested minors. And there were some cases where Church leadership had responded badly. But, after months of coverage, the media seem to have finally accepted the fact that the Catholic priesthood does *not* have a unique problem with the perpetration of child sexual abuse.

It also remains to be determined whether the Catholic hierarchy's response is any worse, compared year to year, than other institutions. Has the Catholic Church been singled out for unfair treatment? The Apostolic Nuncio to the United States, Archbishop Gabriel Montalvo, said in his address to the U.S. Bishops of June 2003: "We all know that we are going through difficult times and that some real problems within the church have been magnified to discredit the moral authority of the church."[61]

These statements are important for the media and society to consider. Nevertheless, as Archbishop Montalvo noted, there are "real problems within the church." The public lashing that we have received these past years, while distorting many of the facts, has not distorted a wake-up call that we should have heard. Perhaps God is using this lashing to deliver a message.

God Turns Disaster Into Grace

It would not be sufficient, I believe, to suggest that the problem is solved if the Church simply dismisses all priests guilty of child sexual abuse and every bishop resigns who has dealt with a case badly. It is a secular model that delineates "good" people from "bad" people, or, in this case, "good" priests/bishops from "bad" priests/bishops. As this thinking goes, once we identify these bad people and get rid of them, everything will be fine. This is not a Christian model.

The question of whether offending priests should be returned to any priestly ministry at all is another question. It is fraught with difficulties and conflicts. I do not venture to give extended thoughts on the subject here. I simply say that the Church has fallen into an impossible conflict. There are compelling reasons *against* "zero tolerance:" it is a one-size-fits all, unjust approach that arguably puts children more at risk by removing the possibility of ongoing monitoring. There are also compelling reasons *in favor of* zero tolerance: For the integrity of its own ministry, for the good of the people, and for the protection of the children entrusted to its care, the Church cannot tolerate the possibility of re-offense nor can it adequately supervise men known to be offenders. The question of return to ministry is incredibly complex from child protection, clinical, legal, and pastoral perspectives, a complexity that has not yet surfaced in the public forum. Many people have strong opinions which they are convinced are completely correct. But when one delves deeply into this issue, one can see how a simple solution eludes us. We might start with recognizing this complexity and having everyone work together to find a common solution. The Dallas decisions will remain open to further scrutiny from the Church and from society as the years pass.

But this recent public verbiage that separates priests into good ones and bad ones is a dangerous approach that reflects a misleading mind-set. I recall an interview of former President Jimmy Carter on public radio after he had received the Nobel Peace Prize. He said that the media tend to paint people as all good or all bad, and that this is an exaggeration that is neither helpful in his work in negotiations, nor is it accurate.

In a Christian approach, we begin with the basic understanding that, while we were all created good by God, we are all sinners, regardless of whether we are powerful or weak, old or young, bishop or laity. The scriptures are clear: "If we say, 'We are without sin,' we deceive ourselves, and the truth is not in us. If we acknowledge our sins, he is faithful and just and will forgive our sins and cleanse us from every wrongdoing" (1 Jn 1:8–9). The Christian approach begins with this understanding of our combined and personal sinfulness and calls each of us to repentance and conversion. Sadly, there has been much finger-pointing during the crisis. Each group blames other groups. Rather, each of us ought to begin by pointing the finger at ourselves and ask, "How did I contribute to this problem?"

This crisis has been a disaster for everyone involved: victims, families, parishes, Church, and perpetrators. And one ought to acknowledge it as a disaster. However, God has the uncanny ability to transform the greatest of disasters into moments of grace. For example, what has been the greatest disaster of all time? The answer is undeniable: the crucifixion of Jesus. God sent his only Son in a total self-gift to humankind. This Son came to bring the life and goodness of God to us. We responded by killing him. We horribly killed God's self-gift to us on the cross. Yet, God transformed this despicable act of humanity into a moment of supreme grace. If such a miracle has been done with the human disaster we call the crucifixion, we can be sure that God can and will do the same with this disaster.

What then is the grace that God will work through this crisis? It is probably too early to tell, and God's intentions always remain somewhat hidden. But it seems likely that one of the graces to come from this tragedy, at least for the Church, will be the renewal of the Church in general, and in particular, a renewal of the clergy. The words of the Holy Father to the American Cardinals gathered in Rome in April 2002, quoted at the opening of this chapter, are important: "This time of trial will bring a purification of the entire Catholic community, a purification that is urgently needed." Moreover, the Holy Father, addressing the bishops of Boston and Hartford, spoke even more directly about the central importance of a renewal of the clergy:

> In a particular way I would ask you to be strongly supportive of your brother priests, many of whom have suffered deeply because of the much-publicized failings of some of the Church's

> ministers. I would ask you also to convey my personal gratitude for the generous and selfless service which mark the lives of so many American priests, as well as my deep appreciation of their daily efforts to be models of holiness and pastoral charity in the Christian communities entrusted to their care. In a very real way the renewal of the Church is linked to the renewal of the priesthood. (cf. Optatam Totius, 1)[62]

Thus, it is our task not to let this moment pass without gleaning the grace that God has in store for us. We ought to pursue vigorously this purification of the entire Church and of the presbyterate.

When I speak of the renewal of the clergy, I do not wish to suggest that we are trying to make an essentially defective clergy into a good one. As was just noted, while the Holy Father himself called for a renewal of the clergy, he also expressed his "personal gratitude for the generous and selfless service which mark the lives of so many American priests." It is true that priests today have their personal issues, as all people do, but it is my experience and my conviction that the priesthood today is a sound one. We have a solid group of men who are dedicated, faith-filled, and, for the most part, psychologically and spiritually strong. In fact, survey research reported in this book continues to show that priests are happy in their ministries and strongly committed to their vocations, despite the pain and suffering they have personally endured during the crisis.

Renewal is not to make a bad priesthood become good; rather, it is to make a strong priesthood even better. The challenge of these materialistic, sex-obsessed, and secular times demands an enormous amount from the priests of today. For a priest today to remain faithful, enthusiastic, celibate, and alive requires a very high level of spiritual depth and psychic maturity. These difficult times demand that priests be more than good. The crucible of these times will propel us into a level of sanctity and commitment that we previously would not have imagined.

This renewal that now thrusts itself upon us might be considered to be multilayered, a threefold renewal for priests and bishops alike. In this threefold renewal, we priests are to be renewed as *Christians*, renewed as *priests*, and renewed as *Christian leaders*.

Renewal as Christians

By the grace of baptism, priests are first and foremost children of God and followers of Jesus, that is, Christians. Not too long ago I was in a seminary and asked the seminarians this question, "Are you a Christian?" Some looked puzzled, others guffawed. But it might be important to pose this question to all our seminarians in the course of their formation: "Are you a Christian?" That is, have you personally been touched by the saving power of Christ? If not, you have nothing to preach and your homilies will be empty regurgitations of theological phrases that you have heard, without personal conviction or passion.

When we minister to others in the name of the Church as priests, we do so first as brothers of the people, as a Christian among other Christians. As Saint Augustine said, "The first aspect is that I am a Christian; the second, that I am a leader."[63] As important as the sacrament of orders is, which we shall address in the next section, our first identity should be as fellow Christians.

After working with a number of priests in difficulty, I am struck by a common perception that many of them have about how the good news applies, or does not apply, to them. Many of these priests in trouble have said to me, "I feel like the good news applies to everyone else but me." Similarly, just a short time ago, I was speaking with a priest who had entered treatment and was doing rather well. He said he had always viewed his role as being someone who led others to Christ but he felt himself an outsider looking in. As treatment progressed, he eventually came to see himself as someone who has been personally touched by the healing love of God.

This is essential for all priests. We must be individuals who personally know the saving grace of Jesus. If we do not, how can we possibly preach and teach the good news with conviction? As noted in the last chapter, when priests complete our program at Saint Luke, they come to know their own vulnerability and sinfulness, and personally experience God's forgiveness. Essential to the renewal of the priesthood is our renewal as Christians. When we have come personally to know our sinfulness and God's forgiveness, there can be no room for arrogance or clericalism. The priest or bishop who has truly become a Christian himself is a humble man who sees himself as a brother to his fellow Christians.

So, this presumes that we are aware of our own sinfulness. Priests who have obvious, serious problems, such as alcohol addictions, depressions, or sexual addictions have the "blessing" of being acutely aware of their human weaknesses and need for God. This renewal of priests as Christians ought to include opening ourselves to the divine grace of knowing our sinfulness and the bounty of God's forgiveness.

I recall a story told many years ago by Trappist monk Thomas Merton. He said to imagine yourself drowning. As you are going down for the third time, you believe that all is lost. Suddenly, a hand reaches down and grabs yours, pulling you to safety. How would you feel? You would be excited. You would be elated. You would be grateful. Merton said that this is the experience of salvation. Unfortunately, Merton added, we do not know we are drowning.

One sure way of cultivating this grace of knowing our sinfulness is frequent and reflective reception of the sacrament of Reconciliation. It is no secret that some priests are lax in their reception of this sacrament. As noted previously, my recent study found that 88.0 percent of priests received the sacrament of Reconciliation within the past year. While it is a strong majority, there are still over 10 percent who did not. And 60.7 percent of the priests said they received this sacrament within the past three months. While yearly reception is the minimum for the faithful, one would expect a priest to receive this sacrament more often. It should be noted that priests cannot be good confessors if they are not good penitents. This is another way of saying that we cannot be good priests unless we are first good Christians. Regenerating our enthusiasm for this sacrament ought to be a priority.

But this knowledge of ourselves cannot end with a consciousness of our sinfulness. It must rise to a joyful awareness of having been personally forgiven and graced by God. Thus, we are excited by the good news. We can stand at the pulpit and preach this wonderful good news with integrity and conviction.

We see a human face like ours when we look upon the poor and suffering, and upon those who have been victimized in any way. It has become painfully obvious during this crisis that, in the past, we had not truly heard the heart-felt cries of the victims. When we know them as our brothers and sisters, vulnerable people like us, we can hear their pain. United as sinners who have been graced by the forgiveness of God, we find ourselves in solidarity with victims as well as in solidarity with perpetrators.

The word that strikes me forcibly in the wake of the crisis is *humility*. The people expect their priests and bishops to be humble. If God is working any grace in the wake of this disaster, certainly a part of it must be making the priests and bishops of this country the humble people that God calls them to be. Humble people are able to hear the cries of the poor and suffering.

Renewal as Priests

When I speak of renewal of priests, I mean both priests and bishops. In the wake of the abuse crisis, there has been a chasm opening between priests and bishops. This is dangerous for Church leadership as well as for the faithful. Bishop Gregory in his 2002 presidential address in Dallas eloquently spoke to priests, saying:

> The Holy Spirit in the Sacrament of Orders unites us to you as our first collaborators in ministry and we love you as brothers. We are also proud of and grateful for the selfless way in which you serve the Lord and your brothers and sisters day after day. We Bishops are . . . sorry that failures in our leadership have led to a breakdown of trust between priests and bishops, brothers in ministry. We ask your forgiveness. I ask our priests to continue to work closely with us; we need you.[64]

Just as the bishop needs his priests, so do we priests need our bishop. And both of us ought never forget that it is from our priestly ranks that our bishops were chosen. It is too simplistic to blame the crisis on the bishops. Rather, we priests should stand in solidarity and support of our bishops and face the difficulty and the blame together. In reality, whatever failings they may have, such failings arise from our ranks.

Nevertheless, one must be careful not to exaggerate the rift between priests and bishops. While this breach is real and deserves our concerted attention, the *Los Angeles Times* 2002 poll showed that the large majority of priests approve of their own bishops. 37 percent said they *strongly* approved of the way their own bishop was handling his duties overall and thirty-seven percent *somewhat* approved. This is a very high 76 percent approval rating.[65] Similarly, as previously noted in my own 2003–2005 survey, 75.4 percent said, "I have a good relationship with my bishop" and 76.7 percent agree with the statement, "Overall, I am satisfied with my bishop." The bond between the priest and his bishop is still relatively strong.

What, then, is this "renewal as priests" that both bishops and priests ought to undergo? It seems to me that our living out of the priesthood tends to vacillate between two poles of the truth: the sacredness of the priesthood and the frailty of our humanity. At one moment, we focus on the beauty and efficacy of the sacramental priesthood. At other times, we become acutely aware of the priest's frail humanity. There are some priests whose teaching and preaching emphasize the former and others who emphasize the latter. Emphasizing the sacred sacramentality of the priesthood, to the exclusion of the frail humanity of the priest, can lead to an aloof clericalism. On the other hand, emphasizing the frail humanity easily overlooks the unique importance and gift that the sacrament of the priesthood is for the people. If the former breeds arrogance, the latter breeds an ecclesial syncretism.

Theologically it is somewhat obvious that the priest is both the bearer of an immense grace, configured to Christ the Head through a profound sacrament, and also the bearer of a very frail humanity. We are, at the same time, both bearers of grace and profoundly flawed. These two are not mutually exclusive nor should they war with each other. Rather, they are mutually complementary and actually reinforce each other. What could be worse than having a "super class" of people, thought to be without flaw, who condescend to bless the people? One might speculate what it would have been like if God had chosen angels to be his priests. No, Jesus chose his personal collaborators from the ranks of the sinful human race. The words of John the Baptist should not be far from the lips of every priest: "I am not [the one] . . . the one who is coming . . . whose sandal strap I am not worthy to untie. . . . He must increase; I must decrease" (Jn 1:21,27; 3:30).

I do not think it is news to suggest that priests are both bearers of an immense grace and also frail human beings. While priests and people both accept this reality on an intellectual level, it is very clear that we have not fully integrated it into our psyche and spirit. We do not know it in our "guts." People are shocked that priests have the same failings as they do, and no one is more shocked than the priests themselves. It is a bitter pill. We all want to believe in something pure and noble. We want to experience it firsthand. We reach out to the priest and, sadly, put our faith in him. Perhaps this crisis can teach us all, especially the priests, that our faith is not in the frail human beings God has chosen as priests, but in the Son of God. In the wake of recent events, many people have remarked that they have done just that.

At the same time, it would be a mistake to miss the important, and truly vital, grace that Jesus offers to us in the priest. I suspect this error has been more common since the Second Vatican Council. The ordained priesthood differs, not just *in degree*, but *in kind* from the priesthood of the faithful. As the grace of the sacrament makes him *in persona Christi capitis*, the priest preaches and teaches with authority. When he leads the people as presider of the Eucharist, when he anoints and reconciles, it is Christ himself who is acting through the priest. If there is a decline in priestly vocations today in some countries, it may be that we have forgotten the critical place of the priest for the People of God.

As bearers of such a noble grace, we are to live the Gospel call with particular zeal and fidelity. It is fitting for such a grace and helpful for its efficacy that this man's life would be totally dedicated to God in a celibate commitment. While not all Roman Catholic priests have been required to embrace celibacy, such as former married Episcopalian priests, the latter ought to be considered exceptions. When a priest commits a sin, any sin, he threatens to obscure for himself and for others the beauty of the sacrament of Holy Orders, and thus the beauty of the faith and the Church.

And yet, it is precisely in such a frail humanity, prone to sin, that God enfleshes the sacrament of orders. Whenever we priests or the people of God look to the priest to be our savior, our gaze must be yanked away from the priest and focused on the one true Savior. If the sacrament of orders enables the priest to confer on the people many graces, it is the "sacrament of his humanity" that leads the people beyond the priest to the person of Christ himself. This is a painful lesson for the priest and for the people. "He [Christ] must increase, I [the priest] must decrease."

This dialectic of grace and sin in the person of the priest continues to challenge us in these modern times. Perhaps because of the complexity of our society, we search for simplistic solutions. Media stories often portray such unreal simplicities. But the truth is complex, dynamic, and challenging. One of the complexities is the priest himself. Called to the heights of sanctity, he will always remain humanly no better than the people he serves. *When he or the people forget either the grace-filled power of his calling or the bitter truth of his sinful humanity, there will be serious trouble in the Church.*

Renewal as Church Leaders

The painful grace of this crisis leads us priests and bishops not only to be renewed as Christians and priests but also to be renewed as Church leaders. Once we have refound our Christian identity as sinful people who have been forgiven and loved by God, once we have been renewed as frail humans who have been entrusted with a grace-filled vocation to priesthood, we are ready to reflect upon the third, but no less important, renewal offered to us today. This is a call to be renewed as Church leaders.

There seems to be the beginnings of a sea change that is being reflected in the kinds of words that Church leaders have been using recently. For example, the Vatican Secretary of State, Cardinal Angelo Sodano, addressed the American Cardinals when they went to speak to the Holy Father in April 2002. The Cardinal's brief statement included a clear challenge to the Church in the United States: "Our task is to reflect on the problems of the present moment with great openness of spirit, knowing that the Church should be transparent."[66] Clearly, at this critical moment, the cardinal was emphasizing two words: *openness* and *transparent*. Is this what we in the United States have been lacking that has helped to precipitate this crisis? I believe it is.

The truth of what most U.S. bishops were doing for the past decade and how they handled most of the cases of abuse was never told in the public forum. The fact is that most bishops since 1992 had markedly improved how the Church addressed cases of sexual abuse. While there were terrible exceptions of which we all have become painfully aware, most priest offenders were not simply shuffled from parish to parish. Most were clinically assessed, engaged in a regimen of treatment, and, as our numbers at Saint Luke Institute suggest, about 60 to 80 percent were returned to what was then considered an appropriate ministry involving supervision with limited or no direct contact with minors. The rest were dismissed from ministry.

Using this approach, very few of those returned re-offended. (For example, a Saint Luke Institute statistical study of 368 residents treated for child sexual abuse from 1985–2004 found that over 95 percent had not relapsed since treatment.)[67] During this decade of the 1990s, Church leaders offered most victims psychotherapy for their healing; some were given monetary settlements to compensate them financially for the harm done. But for those people who considered return to any ministry for offenders as a negligent response, this approach was unacceptable. On the other hand, for those who considered the treatment, monitoring, and ongoing supervision of offenders as the most responsible way of promoting the protection of children, it was a step in the right direction, although not the final word. Regardless of how one perceived this approach, the intense, negative public pressure funneled through the media pressured the bishops to dismantle it.

What became clear was that this story of how the Church had markedly improved its response to the sexual abuse of minors could not be told in the midst of an extremely emotional public outcry. The public found out that bishops had been returning some of these men to ministry and assumed the worst. And there were several exceptional cases such as Boston's John Geoghan and Paul Shanley to confirm their worst suspicions. Once the story took off, it had a life of its own, with its own logic and perspective that, although distorted, could not be altered. No one would listen to Church leaders when they tried to make a dent in balancing the perspective. It was too late.

Cardinal Sodano recommended "transparency" and "openness." This approach to leadership must be ongoing and cannot wait until a crisis erupts. I firmly believe that, had we been in regular communication with the secular authorities and the laity regarding our dealing with the crime of child sexual abuse, this crisis would never have assumed the proportions that it did. The real story was about a leadership that they perceived as secretive, arrogant, and which saw itself as "above the law." I believe this criticism is too harsh, but a lack of real communication breeds suspicion and distrust. It speaks of the need for an ongoing transparency and openness.

Archbishop Harry Flynn, chairman of the U.S. bishops' Ad Hoc Committee on Sexual Abuse, said it clearly:

> The crisis of 2002 had its origins in real mistakes made in the past. These errors included a reliance on secrecy, where transparency was needed, and a failure to take the Catholic people into a bishop's confidence. That failure sparked, in turn, a lack of confidence in a bishop's decisions. By neglecting to tell the whole story ourselves, we allowed others to interpret our actions, often in the most negative light.[68]

Similarly, the 2002 Dallas Charter used a word that has also become an integral part of this sea change. This important new word is: accountability. The Dallas Charter noted: "We [bishops] pledged ourselves to act in a way that manifests our accountability to God, to his people, and to one another in this grave matter."[69] The public demanded accountability from the leaders of the Catholic Church. This is difficult for us since the Church, rightfully and zealously, guards its autonomy in preaching the Word of God and in guarding the deposit of faith. We cannot allow secular authorities to determine what is preached. It is a matter of revealed truth that the bishops of the Catholic Church are the successors of the apostles and preach and teach with an authority given by Christ himself. "Whatever you bind on earth shall be bound in heaven; and whatever you loose on earth shall be loosed in heaven" (Mt 16:19).

But the administrative actions of Church leadership do not have the same protection from secular intrusion as do its teachings on faith and morals. John Paul II recognized the legitimate place of secular authority when he said that the sexual abuse of minors "is rightly considered a crime by society."[70] What is at stake here is not theological truth, but the way in which we interact with society in responding to a crime. While we must protect the important separation of Church and State, the Dallas Charter necessarily emphasized the need for the Church to be held accountable in such a grave matter as the protection of children.

This accountability ought to be present, not only at the diocesan level, but also with our priests in parishes, hospitals, schools, and the like. There has already been a movement in this direction in recent years. Because priests receive their assignments from "above," there is a tendency for the system to foster a lack of accountability in priests' actions and behaviors. There have been a number of post-Vatican II initiatives that have attempted to facilitate communication with and accountability of priests, such as the implementation of parish councils and the written reviews of a pastor's ministry by the people of his parish. Because we are all flawed human beings, we must be held directly accountable for our actions and behaviors. A lack of accountability breeds personal corruption.

In 2004 the Holy Father himself spoke to some bishops of the U.S. about the need for a style of leadership in the Church that includes collaboration and shared responsibility but does not fall prey to Trusteeism or a strictly democratic style of leadership:

> The Synod of Bishops acknowledged the need today for each Bishop to develop "a pastoral style which is ever more open to collaboration with all" (*Pastores Gregis,* 44). . . . Within a sound ecclesiology of communion, a commitment to creating better structures of participation, consultation, and shared responsibility should not be misunderstood as a concession to a secular "democratic" model of governance, but as an intrinsic requirement of the exercise of episcopal authority. . . .[71]

There is much evidence to suggest that the grace of a renewal of Church leadership will necessarily include such concepts as openness, transparency, and accountability. These will be important watchwords for future Church leaders. If not, there will be more crises, perhaps of a different nature and concerning different subjects, but such crises will naturally arise out of suspicion, distrust, and a lack of communication.

Concluding Remarks

It was striking to witness the actions of John Paul II on the eve of the millennium. The Holy Father engaged in a deliberate attempt to foster reconciliation for the wrongful behaviors of past Church leaders. He systematically engaged in a public apology to many groups such as women, the Jewish people, victims of the Inquisition, and the Crusades. It was unprecedented behavior on the part of a pope. I think it was one more marker in a sea change or renewal of the Catholic community.

The Holy Father was leading the way in demonstrating a leadership that was open, accountable, and transparent. A traditional word that might sum up this renewal is a simple one: humility. The pope was showing us how to be humble, which includes recognizing our frail humanity and asking for forgiveness.

None of us expected the crisis that has enveloped the Catholic Church in recent years. It has caused untold pain, discouragement, disillusionment, and suffering. The sexual abuse of minors by anyone, but especially by a priest, is a crime; it is a disaster. And occasions when we as Church leaders have not adequately responded have only compounded the trauma.

But we Christians believe, and have come to experience time and again, that God can and will bring out of disaster much grace. It is precisely in the midst of disaster that Christ's message of hope shines most brightly. If we are willing, these days offer us a chance for renewal, to make a good priesthood and a strong Church community even better. There have been many crises in the history of the Church and each time the Church has emerged more humble and more Christ-like. This time will be no exception.

chapter 13

A Priesthood of Joy

The Church needs joyful priests, capable of bringing true joy to God's people, which is the good news in all its truth and transforming power.[72]

✠ John Paul II

I REMEMBER AN INDIVIDUAL VISITING A SEMINARY FOR THE first time. He had not personally known any Catholic priests or seminarians and was walking into a new environment. Nevertheless, he had some preconceived notions. He stepped into the main hall and spent a few moments observing the people. A look of surprise crept over his face and he said to me as he pointed to the left side of the room, "Are those people over there Catholic priests?" "Yes," I replied. And then, after a few moments of silence, he pointed to the right and said, "And those people over there, they are seminarians?" "Yes," I said again. "Why," he exclaimed with a look of surprise, "they seem happy!" I responded, "I think that they are."

Some people associate piety and priesthood with a rather dour endeavor. It is sometimes a bit comical to see someone, new in the faith, try to appear to be holy. They take on a gaunt and pained expression. They look excessively serious and exhibit an eccentricity or two. However, having eccentricities does not make you holy; it only means that you are eccentric.

As Saint Teresa of Avila prayed and is oft-quoted, "From sour-faced saints, O Lord, deliver us!" Saint Teresa knew well that sanctity does not have a sour face. There are altogether too many in our church whose miserable demeanor and underlying anger masquerade as righteousness. *Anger is a weapon of the evil one and misery is one of his fruits.*

It is true that priesthood is a difficult life. But, as we have heard from the priests themselves, it is an intensely rewarding life. Those who commit themselves to priestly service find it to be a life that offers much satisfaction and a sense that one's life makes a difference in the world. Priests are happy to be priests. It is a gift to the people of God, and it is a wonderful gift for the priest himself. Both are blessed.

But the priestly life offers one more blessing. It is a blessing received by all Christians, of course. However, the priest himself, as a person whose life is filled with the presence of Jesus, is offered this gift in an intensely direct and personal way. Very simply put, it is the gift of joy.

There is no better sign of sanctity, or the presence of the Holy Spirit, than a face transfigured with joy. Recall the fruits of the Holy Spirit. These fruits or signs of the Spirit's presence are: "love, joy, peace, patience, kindness, generosity, faithfulness, gentleness, self-control" (Gal 5:22–23). A joyful countenance is a true sign of sanctity.

I am not speaking of someone with a pleasing personality or a person with a happy demeanor. Rather, joy starts in the center of our hearts, bearing witness that the Spirit resides within. It is subtle, gentle, and almost imperceptible to its bearer. As our life progresses and we journey ever closer to that final union with God, the presence of the Spirit radiates more strongly from the heart. Thus, the love, joy, and peace that shine through our eyes and faces become increasingly bright.

This joy is not a passing emotional state. As human beings who live in a changing world, we experience the highs and lows of daily life. We are elated when happy times come and we are saddened when losses and sorrows visit us, as they inevitably do. There is an old spiritual maxim: Do not let your hearts be too puffed up in times of prosperity or too downcast in times of want. We try to maintain an emotional balance but, as frail human beings, we naturally feel good in good times and bad in bad times. However, this is something different from the joy that the Spirit brings.

The joy of the Spirit is a spiritual reality. It is an enduring presence in the heart that increases as we move ever closer to God. Even in times of sorrow, it is present in the heart, bolstering our flagging spirits. For instance, it was said of Saint Therese of Lisieux while she was dying that her face radiated a sense of joy and peace. This was all the more remarkable since she was dying of tuberculosis and was also going through a terrible period of spiritual trial, some say the dark night of the soul. While she emotionally and physically suffered greatly, her spiritual joy and peace never left.

So, too, with the early Christians who were thrown to the lions in the arena. No doubt they experienced normal human fears and, of course, their physical sufferings were intense. But it was said of them that they went to their martyrdoms singing. It is likely that they sang to bolster their courage. But, I suspect that many of them, like the martyrs down through the centuries, experienced the powerful presence of the Holy Spirit that makes the heart sing. The protomartyr Stephen's face radiated like that of an angel's, even though he was suffering the cruelty of public denunciation and stoning (cf. Acts 6:8–7:60). Joy is a spiritual reality that fills our lives and remains with us, even in the midst of intense sufferings.

The theological text, the *Sacramentum Verbi*, described this coexistence of joy and suffering:

> Paradoxical joy in suffering is based not only on the expectation of salvation . . . but is the expression of the definitive union with Christ in love. Whence the apostle is always full of joy even when most oppressed since it is no longer he who lives but Christ lives in him. . . ."[73]

The indwelling of the Spirit brings us this abiding sense of joy, a true mark of sanctity, even in the midst of suffering.

Our Society Is Angry

People often wonder why there is so much external violence in the world. There is, indeed, much anger in the world. Certainly, much of the violence stems from the anger and frustration in people's hearts. People are frustrated and angry, and they do not know why. Many times, they are not even aware of it. We have become so inured with the anger, sadness, and violence of our dismembered world, we do not realize how far our humanity has fallen.

I remember spending several months with the Carthusian monks in Vermont. The Carthusians live a very austere, demanding life. They wear hairshirts, their beds are straw, there is no meat, they are hermits, and they eat only one meal a day. After finishing several months with them, I went down the mountain and got on a city bus. As I sat there among the people on the bus, I was struck and astounded by the amount of sadness on that bus. I thought to myself, "These people are incredibly sad. I wonder what happened to make them all so sad?" Since the Carthusians do not read newspapers, listen to the radio, or watch television I had been cut off from news of the outside world. I figured something terrible must have happened while I was up on the mountain. But after a few moments, the truth came to me: "Nothing happened to these people. These people are always this sad." But I did not know it until I had experienced true joy. Their eleventh-century founder, Saint Bruno, spoke of the Carthusian life as "peace unknown to the world and joy in the Holy Spirit."[74]

People in our world are angry and frustrated. It is this inner anger and frustration that breeds so much violence. A good image of our society is the ancient symbol of a son of the Greek god Zeus, called Tantalus. For his crimes, Tantalus was chained. Above him were grapes and below him was water. When he was hungry he would reach up for the grapes, but they would recede just out of his reach. When he was thirsty, he would bend down for some water, but it, too, would recede beyond his reach. Thus, he was forever "tantalized." Many people of our world cannot find the inner nourishment for which they desperately long. It is little wonder that they become violent.

Then they search for this fulfillment in all the wrong places. Instead of finding true joy, they try to bolster their hearts with the wrong things. As one alcoholic said, "Everyone asks me about my drinking, but no one asks me about my thirst!" Carl Jung wrote to Bill Wilson, cofounder of Alcoholics Anonymous, about one alcoholic that he was treating: "His craving for alcohol was the equivalent on a low level of the spiritual thirst of our being for wholeness, expressed in medieval language: the union with God."[75]

People try to assuage this longing with all the wrong food. Rather than the Bread of Life, they use alcohol and drugs, sex, food, power, money, and many other worldly things to try to fill the void. These only further frustrate and lead to new problems.

Joy in the Christian Life

Unfortunately, many people do not know that the joy and peace of Christ is what their hearts truly desire. People do not know of the Christian joy in our lives, either because of false impressions or because of our own human failings and limitations. A survey was given to fifth-graders in which they were asked to rank in order the desirability of thirty-five careers. They were given such choices as doctor, teacher, lawyer, and others. They were asked to list in order which ones they most wanted to be. One of the thirty-five vocations listed was saint. Any idea where saint was listed by these boys and girls? It was second to last, thirty-fourth! The only less desirable position was garbage collector. In the minds of many, being a saint is only slightly more desirable than being a garbage collector. When asked why saint was listed so low, the children said that being a saint was a negative, unhappy life.

Perhaps we have so publicized the heroic sufferings of the saints that we have failed to tell people what sanctity really is: living in union with our God of joy and peace. Jesus told us what this life is like, "That my joy may be in you and your joy may be complete" (Jn 15:11).

It is a delusion perpetrated by evil that sin is fun and being good is boring. It is common in our world to speak of a sinful life and behaviors as if they brought happiness, and to think of the Christian life as putting a real damper on happiness. Sometimes it even infects our thinking as priests. I was at a confirmation dinner and speaking with an older priest who was *not* noted for his joyful countenance. We were discussing the early profligate life of Saint Augustine and his later conversion. The older priest then exclaimed, "That's the way to do it, have your fun first and then convert!" What an appalling statement. It suggests that sin is fun and being good is negative. In fact, I have worked with many people mired in problems and sinful behaviors, including priests, and I can only conclude that sinful behavior makes one very miserable. It is true that the "wages of sin is death" (Rom 6:23). And I would add, the wages of sin are misery too. Hell is not a happy place. *The more we sin, the more miserable we become and the more we are already fashioning our own hell.*

It is sad to learn of this negative impression in our society of the Christian life. Perhaps this is one reason we do not have more vocations than we do. People think it is a sad, negative life when it is, in fact, just the opposite. It is our society that is so horribly sad and violent. It is Christ and his Spirit who bring the joy and peace of heart that people are so desperately longing for. As Jesus said, "Peace I leave with you; my peace I give to you. Not as the world gives do I give it to you" (Jn 14:27). We priests must preach this with our lives and with our voices: It is only in Christ that the violence of the world will cease because it is only in him that we find the joy and peace that our hearts long for. We will be frustrated into anger and violence until we find it.

We must first and foremost preach this message with our lives. As the Holy Father urged us, "The Church needs joyful priests, capable of bringing true joy to God's people, which is the good news in all its truth and transforming power."[76] As noted previously, I sometimes tell priests who have suffered for many years from difficulties, "It's not a sin to be happy." By this I acknowledge that they have indeed suffered from depression and inner difficulties, but it is ultimately not God's will that we are mired in such problems. While bearing sufferings patiently can bring much grace and sanctification, ultimately, we will want to invite the healing Christ to bring us his gifts of joy and peace. For he told us: "That my joy may be in you, and your joy may be complete" (Jn 15:11).

The countenance of a happy priest is our best vocational tool. It witnesses to the true Christ and invites others to share in his joy.

Joy in the Scriptures

The unmistakable conclusion to draw after reading the good news is that joy is a major component of welcoming Christ into one's life. The scriptures are filled with the words "joy" and "rejoice." They clearly indicate that joy was one of the hallmarks of the early Christian community.

I offer only a few citations to illustrate this point. In Philippians (4:4), we are admonished, "Rejoice in the Lord always, I shall say it again: rejoice!" Similarly, joy is almost seen as synonymous with faith: "And this I know with confidence, that I shall remain and continue in the service of all of you for your progress and joy in the faith" (Phil 1:25). Joy is closely connected with peace: "For the kingdom of God is not a matter of food and drink, but of righteousness, peace, and joy in the holy Spirit" (Rom 14:17). Joy is closely connected with God's love: "Although you have not seen him you love him . . . you rejoice with an indescribable and glorious joy" (1 Pt 1:8). Even in the very beginning, John the Baptist leaps in Elizabeth's womb for joy when he encounters Christ in Mary. Mary, too, sings her song of joy as a result of the indwelling Christ.

The parable of the buried treasure captures the priestly journey into joy. Jesus said, "The kingdom of heaven is like a treasure buried in a field, which a person finds and hides again, and out of joy goes and sells all that he has and buys that field" (Mt 13:44). This parable illustrates well the Christian life, but I think it is particularly applicable to those who attempt to follow

Christ fully, especially his priests. We might be living our lives somewhat oblivious to the good news. Many of us had other vocations in mind, perhaps some thought of a secular career. Others had considered marriage and a family. But then we stumble across a "buried treasure." The kingdom breaks into our lives, often unexpectedly and perhaps not even consciously searched for. But, there it is. And what a find it is!

In order to enter fully into the kingdom, however, we will need to sell all that we have. We will need to give up everything. We do so out of joy and are thrilled with the exchange. We gave up everything but got so much more in return. We priests give up many good things, but we receive so much more in return. Like the individual who bought the field that contained the buried treasure, we priests got a great deal in exchanging our small human sacrifices for a divine life that we dared not hope for. How blessed we are!

As the *Sacramentum Mundi* noted, "The entire proclamation of the good news is presented in terms synonymous with joy."[77] Sanctity is not a dour affair, but rather a proclamation of joy. Down through the centuries, humankind has longed for joy and peace. When it has not been able to find them, frustration and violence have followed in its wake. Jesus has come, bringing us salvation. In this salvation, we are finally at peace and come to know God's radiant joy.

A Priesthood of Joy

Priesthood is a difficult life. Perhaps all vocations are difficult in this fallen world of ours. But you and I who are priests are acutely aware of our own trials. Priesthood is not only a satisfying and meaningful life, but also there is the sound of joy buried in our hearts that makes us at home wherever we are. Most of the time, this joy is slightly below the surface, out of sight from others and often out of sight from our own conscious selves. But it is there. I think it contributes strongly to the sense of well-being and satisfaction of our priests. Most of us are not aware of how much this abiding inner joy brings us peace and contentment.

There are other times when this joy becomes so strong that it fills us with God's presence in a palpable way. Then Mary's song becomes ours, "My soul proclaims the greatness of the Lord; my spirit rejoices in God my savior" (Lk 1:46–47). These moments remind us of how blessed we are.

Conclusion

I close these reflections on priesthood with a true story about a priest with whom we all can empathize.

He was a seminarian during World War II. He was thrown into a Nazi concentration camp during the war and fortunately survived. He came to the Americas after the war, was ordained a priest, and sent to a new, remote mission. He built a church near a village with his own hands and fished for his food. He said Mass every day and did all that he could to invite the indigenous peoples into his church, but no one ever came. This went on for years. They never set foot in his church, despite all his efforts. Finally, after years of apparently fruitless labor, he journeyed back to the city and asked to see the bishop. He asked the bishop to be transferred and said, "This last Christmas in the parish was more depressing than my Christmas in the concentration camp." The bishop approved his request, but said that it would be necessary for them to journey back to the parish and inform the people that the parish would be closed.

They made the long trek back to the village. Then the bishop and priest stood up in front of the assembled community and the bishop announced that the parish would be closed. To their great surprise, the people strenuously objected. When the bishop asked why they were against it, they again voiced their strenuous objection. The bishop said, "Why? No one ever goes into the church or attends any of its functions. Why are you against closing the parish?"

Finally, the elder of the community spoke. He said to the bishop, "You cannot take away the priest. If you take away the priest, you take away our only light." Surprised and stunned, the priest remained. Eventually, the people began to enter the church and only recently has the priest left the mission for retirement, after many, many years. He did not want to go but he is now elderly. He had to leave because of his deteriorating health and need for care.

My brothers, you are a sign of hope. In a world of darkness, your presence, which is the presence of Jesus, is a light for the world. Despite your frail humanity, or perhaps because of it, the light of Christ shines more brightly.

Thank you for the love and care you have shown to so many of the people. Thank you for bringing Christ to us. Thank you for being God's priests.

I wish for each of you the blessings of Christ's joy. And may the words of Saint Bruno become our own. May God grant us all "peace unknown to the world, and joy in the Holy Spirit."

Endnotes

1. Dean R. Hoge and Jacqueline E. Wenger, *Evolving Visions of the Priesthood: Changes from Vatican II to the Turn of the New Century* (Collegeville, Minnesota: Liturgical Press, 2003), p. 32.
2. There was a total of 1,172 priests in the sample from 15 dioceses. The mean response rate (numbers of priests surveyed versus the total number of priests in the diocese) was 67.1 percent. So, it should be largely representative of the priests of the United States. To collect data on priestly morale, I attended nine diocesan convocations of clergy from September 2003 to January 2004 and passed out a written survey at the opening of these convocations. Attending most of these convocations were a substantial majority of the priests in the dioceses. These gatherings were considered "mandatory" or "strongly encouraged" in most cases. Almost all of the priests who attended filled out the survey. The tenth through fifteenth dioceses mailed out the survey to all their priests between February 2004 and January 2005. In all the dioceses, priests were assured that their responses were anonymous and confidential. The dioceses surveyed ranged from east coast to central to west coast U.S.A. and included some hardest hit by the sexual abuse crisis. The interim results of the survey were reported in *America* magazine on September 13, 2004, with a sample of 834 priests responding from 11 dioceses across the United States.
3. Saint Stephen of Hungary, "Admonitions to His Son," as quoted in *The Liturgy of the Hours*, Vol. IV (New York: Catholic Book Publishing Co., 1975), p. 1329.
4. Hoge and Wenger, pp. 29, 40.
5. Ibid., p. 26.
6. CNN.com, March 24, 2003.

7. Michael Paulson, "Most Catholics in Poll Fault Law's Performance," *The Boston Globe*, February 8, 2002.
8. "Overall, a Boom Time for Seminaries," Zenit.org. April 6, 2004.
9. Saint Augustine, *The Confessions of Saint Augustine,* as quoted in *The Liturgy of the Hours*, Vol. III (New York: Catholic Book Publishing Co., 1975), p. 273.
10. Marian Movement of Priests, *To the Priests, Our Lady's Beloved Sons*, sixteenth English edition (Saint Francis, Maine: Marian Movement of Priests, 1995), p. 568.
11. Dean R. Hoge, *The First Five Years of the Priesthood: A Study of Newly Ordained Catholic Priests* (Collegeville, Minnesota: The Liturgical Press, 2002), p. 13.
12. Reprinted and edited from an article by Stephen J. Rossetti, "Renewed Search for Priestly Identity," *Human Development* 23, no. 2 (Summer 2002), pp. 38–42.
13. Raymond E. Brown, *The Gospel According to John XIII-XXI*, The Anchor Bible Series (Garden City, New York: Doubleday & Company, Inc. 1987), p. 879.
14. Timothy M. Dolan, *Priests for the Third Millennium* (Huntington, Indiana: Our Sunday Visitor, 2000), p. 255.
15. cf. Thomas McGovern, *Priestly Celibacy Today* (Princeton, New Jersey: Scepter Publishers, 1998), pp. 77–78.
16. Paul VI, *Ecclesiam Suam* (August 6, 1964) no. 70, www.vatican.va.
17. The Big Book of Alcoholics Anonymous, fourth edition, published by Alcoholics Anonymous World Services, Inc., New York City, 2001, p. 62.
18. Second Vatican Council, *Presbyterorum Ordinis*, no. 7.
19. Second Vatican Council, *Christus Dominus*, (October 28, 1965) no. 28.
20. *Christus Dominus* no. 16.
21. *Presbyterorum Ordinis*, no. 7.
22. CNN poll.
23. Cardinal Francis George, "Statement of Francis Cardinal George to the Holy Father," Ad Limina visit of bishops from Illinois, Indiana, and Wisconsin, (May 28, 2004), www.vatican.va.

24. Cf. www.Britannica.com under celibacy.
25. In "The Nature and Scope of the Problem of Sexual Abuse of Minors by Catholic Priests and Deacons in the United States," conducted by the John Jay College of Criminal Justice for the U.S. Conference of Catholic Bishops. The committee found that about 4 percent of Catholic priests from 1950–2002 had allegations of child sexual abuse. While no comparable statistics are available for the general population of men in the U.S., there are no indications that this percentage of priests is higher.
26. Robert T. Michael, et al., *Sex in America: A Definitive Survey* (New York: Warner Books, 1994), p. 165.
27. Patrick Carnes, *Out of the Shadows: Understanding Sexual Addiction*, second edition (Center City, Minnesota: Hazelden, 1992), p. 120.
28. Hoge, *The First Five Years*, p. 29.
29. Ibid., p. 64.
30. Ibid., p. 13.
31. Karl Rahner, "The Spirituality of the Church of the Future," in *Theological Investigations* 20, pp. 143–153.
32. Thomas Merton, *The Wisdom of the Desert: Sayings from the Desert Fathers of the Fourth Century* (New York: New Directions, 1960), pp. 441–442.
33. John Paul II, *Pastores Dabo Vobis* (March 25, 1992), no. 43, www.vatican.va.
34. The traits were taken from the Bem Sex Role Inventory. The study was conducted at a priest continuing education workshop with a sample of 115 priests.
35. John Paul II, *Redemptoris Missio* (December 7, 1990), no. 2, www.vatican.va.
36. Congregation for the Doctrine of the Faith, *Dominus Jesus* (August 6, 2000), no. 2, www.vatican.va.
37. Ibid., no. 16.
38. John Paul II, "Ad Limina Talk to the Bishops of San Antonio and Oklahoma City" (May 2004), www.vatican.va.
39. Reprinted and edited from Stephen J. Rossetti, "The Priest as a Man of Communion," *Origins* 32, no. 17 (October 3, 2002), pp. 283–289.

40. *Pastores Dabo Vobis*, no. 43.
41. Avery Dulles, S.J., *A Testimonial to Grace and Reflections on a Theological Journey*, fiftieth anniversary edition (Kansas City: Sheed & Ward, 1996), pp. 133–135.
42. *American Heritage Dictionary*, fourth edition (Boston: Houghton Mifflin Co., 2000), p. 382.
43. Congregation for the Doctrine of the Faith, *Dominus Jesus*, no. 16, www.vatican.va.
44. Hoge and Wenger, pp. 53–69.
45. Reprinted and edited from an article by Stephen J. Rossetti, "Understanding Diocesan Priesthood," *Human Development* 20, no. 1 (Spring 1999), pp. 35–39.
46. Saint Gregory the Great, from a "Homily on Ezekiel," as quoted in *The Liturgy of the Hours*, Vol IV (New York: Catholic Book Publishing Co., 1975), p. 1366.
47. Hoge and Wengler, p. 33.
48. Ibid., pp. 32–33.
49. Reprinted and edited from Stephen J. Rossetti, "From Anger to Gratitude: Becoming a Eucharistic People," *Origins* 33, no. 44 (April 15, 2004), pp. 757–762.
50. Catherine Doherty, an unpublished essay.
51. *Catechism of the Catholic Church* (Washington: USCC Publishing, 1994), no. 1767–1768.
52. Robert A. Emmons and Michael E. McCullough, "Counting Blessings Versus Burdens: An Experimental Investigation of Gratitude and Subjective Well-Being in Daily Life," *Journal of Personality and Social Psychology*, 84, no. 2 (2003), pp. 377–389.
53. Karl Rahner, ed. *Encyclopedia of Theology: The Concise Sacramentum Mundi* (New York: Crossroad, 1986), p. 448
54. Walter Brueggeman, *The Message of the Psalms* (Minneapolis, Minnesota: Fortress Publishers, 1984), pp. 52–53.
55. Thomas Merton, *The Wisdom of the Desert: Sayings from the Desert Fathers of the Fourth Century* (New York: New Directions, 1960), p. 40.
56. Stephen J. Rossetti, *A Tragic Grace: The Catholic Church and Child Sexual Abuse* (Collegeville, Minnesota: The Liturgical Press, 1996), p. 27.

57. Ibid., p. 85.
58. Reprinted and edited from Stephen J. Rossetti, "Renewal of the Priesthood in the Post-Dallas Era," *Origins* 33, no. 15 (September 18, 2003), pp. 241–248.
59. John Paul II, "Address to the Cardinals of the United States" (April 23, 2002), www.vatican.va.
60. Peter Steinfels, "Abused by the Media," *The Tablet*, September 14, 2002, www.thetablet.co.uk.
61. Archbishop Gabriel Montalvo, unpublished address to bishops of the United States, June 2003.
62. John Paul II, "Ad Limina Address to the U.S. Bishops of Boston and Hartford" (September 2, 2004), www.vatican.va. cf. Optatum Totius.
63. Saint Augustine, "On Pastors," in *The Liturgy of the Hours*, Vol. IV (New York: Catholic Book Publishing Co., 1975), p. 255.
64. Wilton D. Gregory, "A Catholic Response to Sexual Abuse: Confession, Contrition, Resolve," presidential address to the bishops of the United States, Dallas, Texas (June 13, 2002), www.usccb.org.
65. Jim Darling Richardson, "Poll Analysis: Priests Say Catholic Church Faces Biggest Crisis of the Century," *Los Angeles Times*, October 20, 2002.
66. Cardinal Angelo Sodano, "Address of Cardinal Angelo Sodano to the Cardinals of the United States" (April 23, 2002), www.vatican.va.
67. Unpublished study by Dr. Stephen Montana, Saint Luke Institute. From 1985 to 2004, 368 priests who have sexual interest and attraction to minors completed treatment at the Institute. Of these 368, 16 of them relapsed after treatment, a 4.3 percent relapse rate. Relapse was defined as sexual touch of a minor. Most institutions studying child abuse relapse use rearrest rates. Saint Luke Institute used rearrest rates plus other sources of information including self-report, reports of new complaints, and information from religious superiors and supervisors so its data are likely to be more complete.

68. Archbishop Harry J. Flynn, "What Has the Charter Accomplished?" *America* 191, no. 11 (October 18, 2004), p. 9.
69. *Charter for the Protection of Children and Young People* (Washington: USCCB, 2002), p. 3.
70. John Paul II, "Address to the Cardinals of the United States."
71. John Paul II, "Ad Limina Address to the U.S. Bishops of Pennsylvania and New Jersey" (September 12, 2004).
72. John Paul II, Address at Vespers at St Joseph's Seminary, New York (October 6, 1995).
73. Johannes B. Bauer, ed., *Encyclopedia of Biblical Theology: The Complete Sacramentum Verbi* (New York: Crossroad, 1981), p. 441.
74. Saint Bruno's Letter to Raoul Le Verd, in *Carthusian Way of Life*, unpublished ms. (Arlington, Vermont: Charterhouse of the Transfiguration, 1987), p. 24.
75. C. G. Jung, Letter to William G. Wilson (January 30, 1961).
76. John Paul II, Address at St Joseph's Seminary.
77. Karl Rahner, ed. *Encyclopedia of Theology,* p. 439.

FR. STEPHEN J. ROSSETTI is a priest of the Diocese of Syracuse, New York. He graduated from the Air Force Academy in 1973 and spent six years in the Air Force as an intelligence officer. After ordination, he served in two parishes before becoming Director of Education of the House of Affirmation. He is author of the Paulist Press bestseller *I Am Awake* and Twenty-Third Publications' *Fire on the Earth.* He is editor of the Silver Gryphon Award-winning book *Slayer of the Soul: Child Sexual Abuse and the Catholic Church* and author of *A Tragic Grace*, released from Liturgical Press.

Fr. Rossetti is currently the president and chief executive officer of Saint Luke Institute in Silver Spring, Md., a residential treatment program for clergy and religious men and women. A licensed psychologist in the states of Maryland and Massachusetts, he holds master degrees in psychology, political science, and theology. He has a Ph.D. in psychology from Boston College and has a Doctor of Ministry degree from Catholic University. Recipient of a Proclaim Award by the USCCB, he was also a member of the National Conference of Catholic Bishops' Think Tank on Child Sexual Abuse and was a founding board member of

the Saint John's University Interfaith Sexual Trauma Institute. He is presently a consultant to the USCCB Ad Hoc Committee on child sexual abuse. Fr. Rossetti lectures and gives workshops to clergy and religious in several countries on such topics as:

- spirituality
- psychosexual development and integration
- wellness
- sexuality
- mental health

He has authored many articles on these issues.

On April 2, 2000, Fr. Rossetti received the Distinguished Priest Award from the John Carroll Society of the Archdiocese of Washington, D.C., for his significant contribution to health care ministry.

The bibliography of his works is also on the website sli.org.

Alter Christus

St. Paul Speaks to Priests

John J. Gilchrist

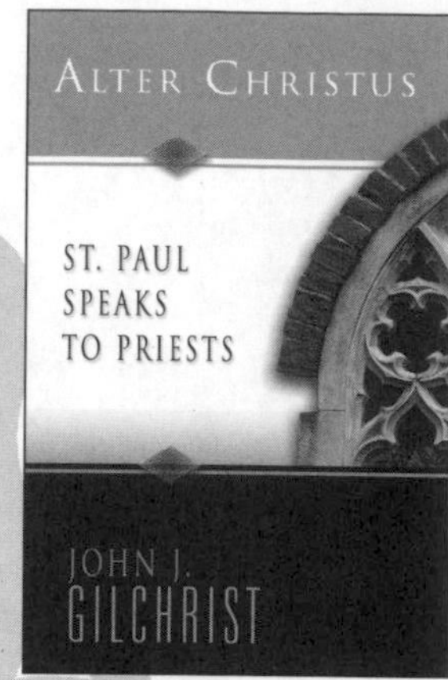

Drawing on the words of St. Paul and a lifetime of pastoral experience, Msgr. Gilchrist provides spiritual sustenance for priests of all ages and ministries. Personal and prayerful meditations touch on subjects that are at the heart of the daily life of a priest.

ISBN: 1-59471-031-7 / 288 pages / $14.95

Can You Drink The Cup?

138,000 sold!

Can we drink this cup as Jesus did? Henri Nouwen not only raises that question but also wrestles with it on every page. With stories from his family life and his life with people with mental disabilities, he challenges us to drink our cup to the bottom, thereby letting it become the cup of our salvation.

ISBN: 0-87793-581-5 / 112 pages / $10.95

When the Lion Roars

A Primer for the Unsuspecting Mystic

Stephen J. Rossetti

Becoming a mystic is not a matter of learning some "mystical secret," but of entering into the divine simplicity of God's unbounded and unrestrained love. Addresses questions and concerns that arise on the path to deeper prayer.

ISBN: 0-87793-985-3 / 160 pages / $11.95

KEYCODE: FØAØ1Ø5ØØØØ

Prices and availablity subject to change. Available at your local bookstore, or online retailers, and from **ave maria press** at **www.avemariapress.com** or **1-800-282-1865**.